SIGNS/ & SIGNALS:

The Daybooks of Robert Crosson

SIGNS/ & SIGNALS:

The Daybooks of Robert Crosson

*   *   *   *

Edited by Guy Bennett and Paul Vangelisti
with an Introduction by Guy Bennett

OTIS BOOKS / SEISMICITY EDITIONS
The Graduate Writing program
Otis College of Art and Design

Archive for New Poetry
Mandeville Special Collections Library,
University of California, San Diego

LOS ANGELES ● 2008

*The editors would like to thank Sarah Suzor
for her assistance on this book.*

Book design and typesetting: Rebecca Chamlee

ISBN-13: 978-0-9796177-3-7
ISBN-10: 0-9796177-3-1

OTIS BOOKS / SEISMICITY EDITIONS
The Graduate Writing program
Otis College of Art and Design
9045 Lincoln Boulevard
Los Angeles, CA 90045

www.otis.edu
www.gw.otis.edu
seismicity@otis.edu

Available from:
SPD / Small Press Distribution
1341 Seventh Street
Berkeley, CA 94710
800.869.7533
www.spdbooks.org

Introduction

ROBERT CROSSON WAS A PROLIFIC WRITER, though you would never know this if you considered only his published books: five slim volumes of poetry and one autobiographical miniature in a career that spanned some 40 years. As with Borges' Menard, however, it may well be that Crosson's most compelling work never saw the light of day. Nor was it intended to, for from September 1957 up to his death in December 2001, Crosson filled more than 100 large-format notebooks – "daybooks" as he called them – with a rich body of writing and a variety of related materials intended apparently for a single reader: himself.

Patiently and diligently compiled over many years, the daybooks include writings both diaristic and literary, collages, doodlings, correspondence, photographs, diagrams of carpentry jobs and estimates for work, fliers for and notes on poetry readings, performances, and other events that he participated in or attended, programs of music recitals and concerts he heard, press clippings on the events or other creative projects in which he was involved, etc. These encyclopedic yet personal books are much more than a writer's journal – they are the material "proof" of his existence, the factual, concrete record of his daily physical and intellectual life, and as such, much more than his published titles, they constitute his life's work.

Crosson began keeping the daybooks while in his twenties and continued to do so for the rest of his life, the last entry dating from the day before he died on December 10, 2001 at 72. As he moved from place to place the growing collection of black-bound volumes moved with him, growing more and more numerous over time. In his later years, they filled the shelves that lined the walls of his tiny converted-garage apartment, and after his death they were donated to the Mandeville Special Collections Library of the University of California, San Diego, where they can be found today, chronologically organized in twenty-nine archival boxes.

There are a total of 117 daybooks. The first is dated September–October 1957 (mysteriously, it is listed as "book 4," suggesting that three other daybooks preceded it and have subsequently been lost), the last one May–June 2001. Shortly thereafter Crosson was hospitalized as a result of a stroke-like accident that left him immobile but not inactive. While in the hospital he continued writing; as he was without his usual notebooks, he filled stacks of 3" × 5" note cards, and when those ran out, he wrote on blank envelopes. A single 8 ½" × 11" notebook also dates from this period. These materials were presumably all he had to write on at the time, and it is possible that he intended to copy these final entries into proper daybooks when he returned home, though he never did.

Taken as a whole, the daybooks fall into three broad groups. The first spans the years 1957–1979, documenting the first twenty-two years of Crosson's activity as a writer, at first of fiction, then of poetry. The second group covers the following nineteen years 1979–1998, covering the most mature and productive phase of his career as a poet, as well as the beginning of his decline. The third and final group of daybooks and related materials mark the period – from late 1998 to late-2001 – at which Crosson essentially abandoned poetry for the visual arts, specifically collage, which occupied the final years of his life.

Early Daybooks (1957-1979)

As if reflecting his tentative beginnings as writer, the first daybooks, fourteen in all, are of varying shapes and sizes. Some of them are student notebooks with lined pages and pre-printed folios, others are small format "books" with unlined, unnumbered pages. Crosson filled all of these volumes with a neat, flowing script, writing in either pen or pencil on one or both sides of the page.

The earliest daybooks are predominantly diaristic, and focus on the basic events of their author's day to day life: the friends he saw, the places they went and things they did, the meals they shared, etc. Soon enough, however, the books would incorporate a variety of other information and materials: letters he had written and received, accounts of dreams he had had, comments on the books he was reading and music he was listening to, etc. He also recorded his thoughts about writing, his own and the writing of others, and occasionally quoted passages from his readings.

Of course, the daybooks also include passages of texts he himself was working on at the time, prose fragments at first, but also dramatic sketches and, infrequently, poems. Beginning in the early 1970s, the daybooks come to feature more and more poetry, occasionally even haiku, as well as notes on stanzaic structure and rhyme schemes, and lists of rhyming words. This early poetry is very personal, seemingly drawn from life experiences: encounters with lovers, descriptions of nature, etc.

In later years Crosson would return to these earlier daybooks, at times appending new writings to them, cross referencing a given page to others in the same volume, and drawing from the literary texts for later works. In one daybook from the 1960s, for example, a passage from Dorothy M. Richardson's *Pilgrimmage* that Crosson had pasted to the page was later appropriated for his radio play *Party: A Reunion* (aired live on KPFK, on November 23, 1977), while other passages were undoubtedly cannibalized in his sprawling, still unpublished novel *Roundtrip to Midland*.

Mature Daybooks (1979–1998)

While Crosson's early daybooks appeared only sporadically, with months or even years going by without a book to mark them, from late 1979 he began to write continuously, filling anywhere from two to six volumes per year. For most of that decade, he gave titles to each of the daybooks (the last one being "Signs/ & Signals" of October–December 1989); all of the others are untitled.

Gone are the prose and dramatic texts that appear in the earlier daybooks; from this point on, poetry predominates. It is composed in his "mature" style, featuring (frequently numbered) stanzas of varying lengths set at different indents, giving the text the architectonic quality that characterized his poems. These daybooks are also peppered with rub-on letters, photographs, and postcards that Crosson collaged onto the pages, revealing a familiarity with concrete and visual poetry that he undoubtedly encountered through Paul Vangelisti, a longtime friend and benefactor, and the latter's magazine *Invisible City,* and that foreshadow his later interest in the visual arts.

In fact, it appears that during this period Crosson began considering the daybooks as works unto themselves, perhaps even as *a* work, since he frequently referred to them in the singular (i.e. as "Daybook"), suggesting that, in compiling these volumes, he was creating a single, *roman fleuve*-like work of which he was the protagonist and whose plot traced the meanders of his own life. In the untitled volume dated June–July 1990, there is a revealing passage which supports this interpretation. In it, Crosson refers to a manuscript (coincidentally called *Daybook* itself) that was languishing at the publishers, then in the very next sentence speaks in more general terms about the collective work which bears the same name:

> *Daybook* yet lingers at Red Hill. (By this time – some years later, it is yet to come into print.)... what I was (am) doing in Daybook, is exactly what you say: 'publishing' my own book, in pencil... which is not to say it's hot-stuff, but what I daily do to make 'sense' of what's otherwise – 'making a living': which is what we all do anyway –. I guess that's maybe (all) any poet can do.? [*reproduced on p. 123*]

The conjunction of writing and life is evident in several other passages, for example in a note penciled into the margins of a poem by Cid Corman that Crosson pasted into the daybook dated December, 1999, and which appears as the epigraph to this introduction. [*It is reproduced on p. 217*] Crosson circled the second stanza which reads, "There's so much to do / about doing nothing and / it takes a lifetime," marked it with an asterisk, then commented parenthetically: "(*viz: 77+ volumes of (ongoing) '*Daybooks*'.) !!?"

Final Daybooks (1998–2001)

In this last period the daybooks undergo somewhat of a transformation, becoming less writerly and more visual in both their content and composition. Perhaps not coincidentally, this change occurred shortly after the June 1998 accident that left Crosson incapacitated and convalescing for nearly three months. Poems appear less and less frequently, as if Crosson were changing gears and/or careers, moving away for whatever reason from verbal expression and toward visual exploration through the creation of abstract collages and, to a lesser degree, drawings and paintings. Curiously, he seems to have developed an interest in Suprematism at this time, and these final daybooks contain many references to Malevich and reproductions of his work. The approximately 300 collages that date from this period are also in the Archive For New Poetry at UCSD.

These final daybooks are all very similar in their layout and organization: each day begins on a new page, with the day and date noted at the top. Beneath these there is a horizontal rule and an ornate, hand-drawn vertical rule marking the left margin. Times of the day are indicated on that rule or just next to it and enclosed in a circle, with horizontal and diagonal lines dividing the page into sections for each entry which primarily related the author's daily activities. Rare indeed are literary texts, and many if not most of these are old pieces that have been recycled here. There is little to no new writing, and no indication of Crosson's former activity and preoccupations. The only writing he seems to have continued is the diaristic chronicling of the daybooks themselves, and this had started to weigh on him, as he wrote in the following lines from April, 2000:

> I, more-and-more – begin to think these 'daybooks' have (to
> me) become a 'pain-in-the-ass' ~
> : an 'unnecessary' "tribute" to the – usual – "Mundane."
> (for-the-moment – however –; some – relentlessly "persist,"
> "as – Document"
> (of what????)))

Commenting on Crosson's shift away from poetry, Vangelisti has suggested that he simply had nothing more to write about, since after his accident he stopped frequenting the Los Feliz bar where he typically spent his days and that had often provided him material for his work. It is also possible that the accident – which may have included a stroke, and which at any rate resulted Crosson's being heavily medicated against the DT's – might have also impeded his working again in language. Whatever the case may be, it is somewhat surprising that after three decades writing poetry, Crosson was able to walk away from this pursuit and not look back. Again we note the parallel between his life and writing: as he declined physically, so too did the daybooks wane. After years of writing in large format notebooks, the final months' entries were written in an 8½" × 11" notebook, and in the end scrawled on 3" × 5" note cards.

Nowhere in the 117 volumes is there any indication as to what moved Crosson to keep the daybooks. According to Vangelisti Crosson was self-obsessed, not out of egotism, but from a desire to know himself and understand his life, and writing for him was a means to achieve that goal. As he grew older, and especially after his accident, the daybooks also served as a memory aid. At one point during his recovery, for example, he wound up back in the hospital. "How did I get here??," he wonders, "When I get home [at issue] and look at 'Daybook,' I can (perhaps) 'find-out'...))."

The daybooks' most significant function, however, was that of a laboratory or quarry for his work: texts were sketched out there, refined, rewritten, and later drawn from to form new pieces or culled for collections. They mingled on the pages with the minutia of his daily life, which also occasionally found its way into his work, perhaps the most successful fusing of the two being his still-unpublished manuscript "Daybook," in essence a distillation of the daybooks into a single, pocketable volume. Given the central place they hold in Crosson's body of writing, we felt it appropriate to highlight them in this way.

As it would have been neither practical nor desirable to reproduce all of the daybooks, nor, we felt, sufficiently representative to publish just one in its entirety, we opted for a middle course. The present volume thus contains one page from each of the 117 daybooks, as selected by Paul Vangelisti and myself during five or six visits to uc San Diego's Archive For New Poetry in the spring of 2006. Though our selection was essentially intuitive – we chose the pages we found most interesting – we did try to give an idea of the daybooks as a whole. We hope that the following pages will shed some light on this unfortunately little-known Los Angeles poet and rekindle interest in his work.

Guy Bennett
Los Angeles – Paris, 2007

SIGNS/ & SIGNALS:

The Daybooks of Robert Crosson

Untitled
September – October, 1957
[MSS 0587   15   5]

A cold mist is coming in, and no John & David!!! Besides, my feet are killing me!!
Lots and lots of pretty whores in Nice -- all very near Ruhl and Astrid. They stand in doorways, just like in the movies (!!)
Orlene is terribly crippled, but so Paul! I like her.
There is a French word for "French always coming out on top."
Orlene thinks we live in a whorehouse. (It's so cheap.)
Perhaps I should lecture and tell the American public outrageous lies, like Michael. --

October 12, 1957 - Barcelona.

I must bridge the gap from Nice to here, later. Barcelona makes me feel more at home than I ever did at home.
A man just locked his door & strolls down the dark labyrin-
thine hallway to the bathroom - in his shorts, straps-flapping. Bells ring everywhere this morning. Olive oil wafts into my narrow-blue-green room from kitchen below: I don't think I'll have breakfast here today, even if I am paying for it. The coffee tastes like watered-mud and the butter like lard. -- Generally, aside from the restaurant where we ate first nite with Marcel (Cochinole??) the food by contrast to France, is nowhere. (LETTER TO JACK LARSEN.) Most beautiful flamenco singing echoes in my room --seems to come from somewhere near the church. God, it is the end --real flamenco singing! And now more spanish music from somewhere else --how I love love love Spain!!! On train to Barcelona from Nice was a grubby spaniard standing by open window. He found reason other than to express himself, started to sing a hoarse flamenco. The French paid him little mind & the man was quite free to be an individual in true French manner--BUT--in Spain everyone sings--

Untitled
1960 – 1961
[MSS 0587   15   6]

chats about women, marriage, old age, and the long-gone days in Chicago. Home at 11³⁰ with Harry (?).

Harry just left.

Tomorrow (at 8) I begin college once again. Ten years it's been, and I am not at this moment overjoyed at the prospect of attending classes, esp. the class in "educational psych" (whoever heard of that?) which I have 5 days a week at 8 am. Returning to my old job at the library I am not at the moment fretting about; that will manage nicely I hope). It's educ. psy. that now lies uppermost in my mind -- that, and the dark dogs that yap in the gulley, and Ortega y Gasset, and the cup of "no-caf" Siesta Coffee I am now determined to drink, ~~~~~~~ no matter what the consequences.

John visits David.

At this very moment everyone I know is drinking at the Carrousel. Me? I'm martyred, for now I am a student. Discipline. ~~That's~~ That's the way with martyrs; they work hard. To be a real martyr you have to sleep a lot. It's an early martyr that ~~~~~~~ gets to catch the worm.

I'd like to go roller-skating.

6-20-60 6am (line from a dream): Love, in

Untitled
1960 – 1961
[MSS 0587   15   6]

following pages: *Untitled*
May – June, 1961
[MSS 0587   15   7]

A. "It is terribly difficult to write with a lighted cigarette."

B. "Aye, that would be true."

C. "I now hear French music. An accordian playing sidewalk music."

A. As usual, you are hearing things."

B "Aye."

C. I don't usually like accordians.

A. nor saxophones.

C. Certainly not with a symphony orchestra. They sound so vulgar. They were all the rage in the thirties.

A. You don't hear saxophones then?

C. I didn't. In those days I wasn't aware of many fine distinctions.

A. Of course not. who was?

B. Aye, who was?

A. I remember too much about it. I remember too much. My memory is a catalogue of all things that happened then.

C. what did happen?

A. I Remember so much I have forgotten most of it. The broad outlines I have more or less forgotten. I once laughed upon arising, I remember that. The play was when I would lie in bed with so much excitement for living that it would stick in my throat.

"Yeah."

"I can't hear you," darling"

bath cheeks, just above along the strong
bold line of his chin. His whiskered beard
was white, and stubbled. He was unshaven,
his beard stiff and peppery.

"Is it fixed?" he asked,

"I said— "He just left."

"   oh."

"   ,

"   "

His accent was
thickly British.

"I know."
"is
ain't it?"   "Christ, you're deaf. Why the hell
are you so deaf, Paul?"

"The war."

"   " "I don't believe it."

I dawdled in the doorway, twisting and
untwisting my fountain-pen.

"It's quite true."
He turned away from the sunlight
and began to stare into space
He seemed to be looking at the folded letter
that lay on the shelf above his typewriter.
"Am I disturbing you?"
"What?"

Untitled
May – June, 1961
[MSS 0587   15   8]

She shrugged again. "—The right place, the right time ..."

Fade out: (over)
        Not Jean. ~~How~~
        How peculiar ...

BOOK TWO

<u>The Carousel</u>; ~~and a description~~

(not a description, not setting scene — no scene to follow, just description, a recollection, a history of times not yet finished, still going on in other places, the same crowd, a semblance of the 'old Carousell scene, but not the same, never the same scene, only ~~cheap~~ imitations of what used to go on at the Carouce, the days of the dancing, before ~~it~~ the place was closed, and ending an unique era in some ~~lives, matter goes description anyway~~ special lives — not a discription, just going back, explaining a few things :)

Jack Larson first took me there.

Jack Larson; an actor — not once have we ever spoken of acting, the art of — not like most, smiling without the shop-talk.

Did I read books? ~~on the~~

on the set, between takes. He was the star. I was a bit. And I was flattered.

Did I read books?

I did.

What books? Not idly, but with peculiar intensity, neither gauche nor

Untitled
June – July , 1961
[MSS 0587   15   8]

sidered a Nazi and who now denies it, said that
Hitler overstepped himself.

"He underestimated democracy," the Herr
Professor explained. "———"

Birds are green and blue
they sing occasionally
in their cage:
white, as the color ('———')

And
as usual
on such oddities
arising ('———')

       invariably
one is, moved to
cosmic philosophy.

(•)

   At such times it is best
to spot ageless ambiguities
    ———

   that is

to stop writing

One is too tired.   Sincerely,   ."

Untitled
August, 1961
[MSS 0587   15   9]

5.00 - Nick Barries

5.15- The Taylors depart. B & I drive to market & pick up my car (left in Thrifty lot the night before).

5:30 I reach home; help Stanley get his stuff in my car. To Von's.

5:40 Von's. Stush moves in. Drinks to celebrate.

7:30 Party breaks up. Stush & I to Thrifty's for dinner.

8:00. Stush home to Von's. I to work.

9:00- work - scouring stone.

11:30 - il. Bal arriving visits shortly. off.

12:30 ◊ Bal arrives. work finished. Bring scotch.

12:30 Drink scotch. Talk.

3:00 Party breaks up. I home to shower.

3:15 Shower. Down to Huffs.

3:30. Huffs. Have sandwich.

4:00 I leave Huffs. Meet Bal, say goodnight.

4:15 home to bed.

up at one today. Call from Stanley. Make tea. Prepare to write

Untitled
October – December, 1961
[MSS 0587   16   1]

11-16-61

1) SHINE YOUR SHOES
AND DINE WITHOUT THEM...

2) LIKE DICKENS,
MAYBE DOSTOEVSKY

11-18-61 : (Friday.) A COLD NIGHT IN CALIFORNIA

Von accuses Mickel of being amoral. We had a long talk about it last night after work. Mike, Von maintains, is a Balkan and as a Balkan shares the Balkan's traditional contempt of women. A woman, to Mike, is a slave who cooks, irons shirts, makes money, and makes love. Since Mike is a Balkan, Von continues, he is not to be judged by American standards of morality; an American, in his disrespect of woman, would be, in Mike's shoes, immoral; an American man who slapped his wife in public, who cursed her in public, or who made love to her in the kitchen of a restaurant, in full view of, and being oblivious to, the entire kitchen staff, would, according to Von, be committing an immoral act. Americans, in short, have a conscience in such matters, whereas the Balkans do not. Unlike the Balkans, Americans are brought up that way. A Balkan treats his wife like dirt; that's the Balkan way of doing things. From an American point of view, a Balkan should be considered, not immoral, but amoral. Von finds immorality, much more acceptable.

Even if Von had a wife, which he doesn't, he would not hit her in public. Nor would he publically make love to her. "I'm not that the kissy type," said Von...

Something was missing somewhere, but I was too tired to fret about it. I drank my drink, said goodnight. My apartment was freezing. I called Stanley's mother: "Stush phoned me tonight from Chicago," I told her. "... Yes, he sounded fine. He'll be in Chicago until the weekend, then he takes off for New York... Yes, he had five dollars, he said... To hell

Untitled
February – December, 1962
[MSS 0587   16   2]

22-1-'63: Tuesday.

<u>BED</u> *

{ VELVET PILLOWS, TWO,
{ SPEAK FROM ——

LAMB'S HAIR, WOVEN, STRETCHED ON A RACK,
DRIED IN MEXICAN SUN, SCRUBBED, WOUND AND BEATEN,
LAMB'S HAIR. BRISTLES ~~UPON~~ ON THE BACK
OF LOVERS, LOCKED IN ~~IT~~ SIDE, WITH THEIR FEET IN.
I SHEARED THE FRINGE,
~~To keep from registering,~~
SHEARED
~~OUT~~ IT OFF ON THE ~~ONE~~ ENDS...
* (LOVE BENDS, WITHOUT REASON...)

THE BED CALLS:
<u>WHERE WILL LOVE COME TODAY?</u>
(BITS OF CLAY
FALL OUT OF IT — FALL
AS CRACKER-CRUMBS,
DUST-BALLS,
PEANUT SHELLS, AND ONE
DEAD GERANIUM.)
THE BED CALLS:
<u>WHERE IS LOVE TODAY?</u>

<u>IT LEFT, I SAY;</u>
LOVE CAME ON CLAY FEET,
WOUND ITSELF UP WITH ME,
~~mmmmmmmm~~ DEEP IN LAMB'S ~~cover~~ VIGOR,
~~and sighed.~~ LOVED-IN TO MEET
LOVE'S ALL IT COULD. AND DID. THEN WENT AWAY —
IT ~~love~~ WENT, ~~the~~ SAD CLAY FIGURE ~~that~~ LIKE NIOBE,
ALL TEARS.

* (while waiting for Ed to
call me from the hospital.)

Untitled
April, 1966 – January, 1967
[MSS 0587   16   3]

or Dr. Johnson: " ... I cannot hope to satisfy those, who
are perhaps not inclined to be pleased, since I have not been
always able to satisfy myself."

Trees & flowers & grass around you —

an unusual location

<u>no</u>   neon

A menu to intrigue you

Monday:	Chicken alla Cacciatora Lasagne al Forno	Friday:	Spaghetti a Sugo Russian Dinner Spaghetti-Clam Sauce
Tuesday:	Chicken Livers Saute Szekely Gulyas	Saturday:	Beef Gulyas Wiener Schnitzel
Wednesday:	Chicken Paprikas Welsh Rarebit		Steaks and Baked Potatoes at Any Time
Thursday:	Stuffed Cabbage Roast Beef		

Austrian - Hungarian, Italian Cuisine

Get away from
for a quiet lu

SIDEWAL

open
noon
'till
midnight
friday
and
saturday
'till
1:o'clock
A.M

sample
FŪREDI BŌZSI'S
fabulous
Vienese pastries

von's
CAFE GALLERIA

A WORLD IN ITSELF APART

Afternoon   coffee & desert

After the theater:
Buffet sandwich bar
& your favorite coffee

Classic Guitar friday & saturday evenings by JEAN H

Mr. v "Larson has brought
Carl

Untitled
February–July, 1967
[MSS 0587   16   4]

['SAVE THE OLEKENOLE .']

'SPOOKED' – PETER – : 'BAD VIBRATIONS'.
ET AL.

        *

        DEAD   DIE,

        *

    (DIONYSIUS .)

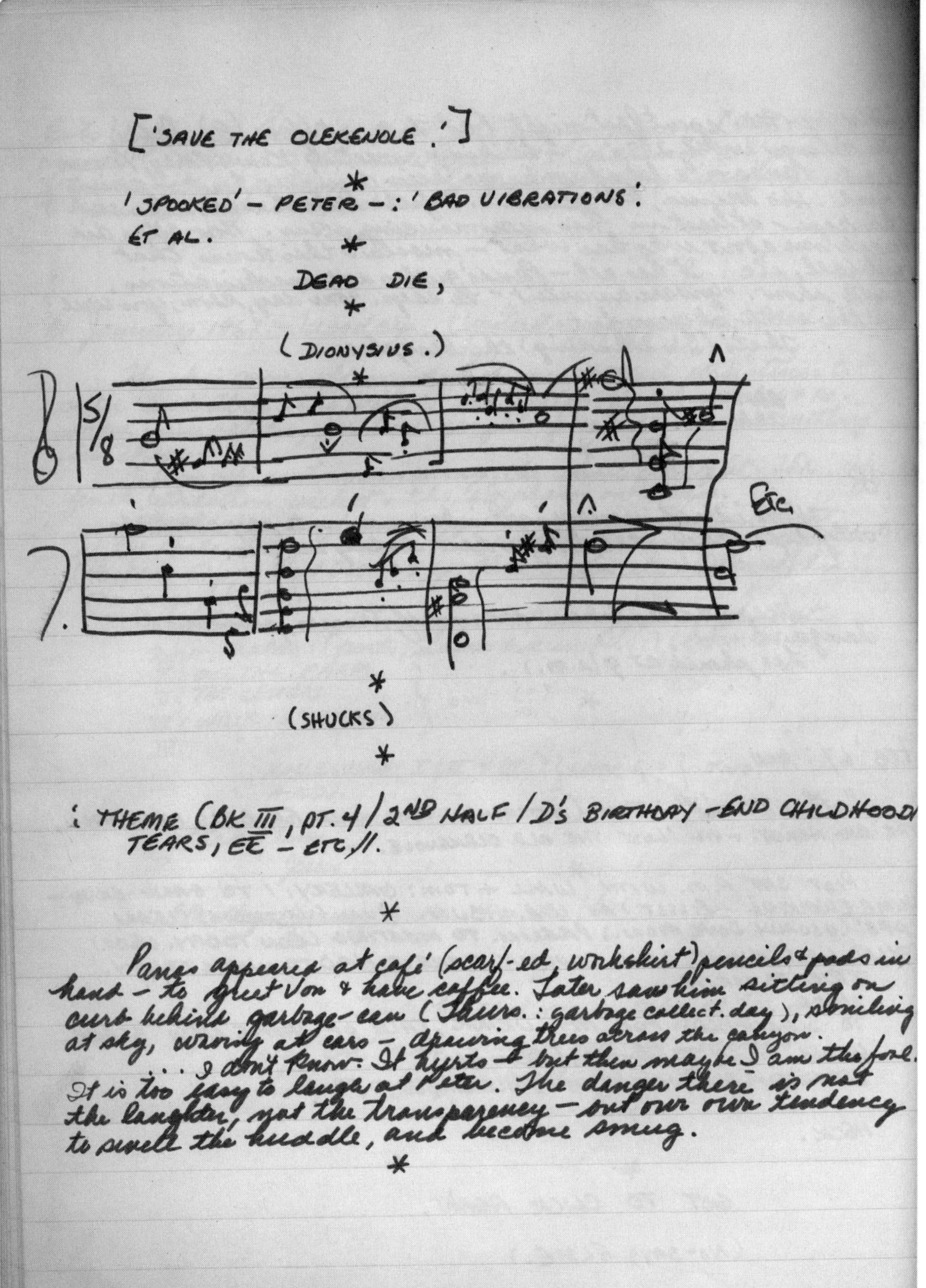

    (SHUCKS)

        *

: THEME (BK III , PT. 4 / 2ND HALF / D's BIRTHDAY – END CHILDHOOD/
    TEARS, EE – ETC./).

            *

  Panos appeared at café' (scarf-ed, workshirt) pencils & pads in
hand – to greet Von & have coffee. Later saw him sitting on
curb behind garbage-can (Thurs.: garbage collect. day), smiling
at sky, waving at cars – spacing these across the canyon.
  . . . I don't know. It hurts – but then maybe I am the fool.
It is too easy to laugh at Peter. The danger there is not
the laughter, not the transparency – but our own tendency
to swell the huddle, and become smug.
            *

Untitled
July 1967 – January, 1969
[MSS 0587   16   5]

attitudes without understanding why our private gestures are, at last, perhaps not ours, unique; for, at last, and looking back we see that we all had a share in it: Stein, D. M. Richardson, Proust, me and, likewise, the lesser, a row of others who wrote, the clerics, long-jawed, ~~[crossed out]~~ in a spasm of compunction. we were bent in the same direction by genes, public temper, ourselves, our fits and fights and private circumstance. Yes? —? (↓)

I like the stillness of deserts very much. The page is written with a ball-point pen I use for carpentering. The page is clipped with T-square (bottom) and a Sears-Roebuck stapling gun. I haven't written in too long. And to hell with it except I can't always say that. Pastures change. Some last very long. I wish I could remember the simple things. Jumbo wants to go to Jon's house tomorrow, to get a hanging lamp, a vase and a blue mirror. Irma, whom I was to see today, saves me a piece of litmus paper so I can piss on it and see if I have sugar-diabetes. The boys, the new owners, want me on as a p-r man, so I can soothe the neighbors. . . . "Its inhumanity was the only moral issue which impeded her. Like the past and the present, places and persons could not stay together. It was impossible to be with both, and impossible to choose to be with persons. But not to choose to be with them was perilous; and perhaps evil." (†M. Ellmann) [Italics mine]

"Yes would be a lie. No would be a lie. Any statement would be a lie. All statements are lies. I like the Pernes better than I like you. I like all of you better than the Pernes. I hate you. I hate the Pernes. I, of course you must know it, hate everybody. I adore the Pernes so much that I can't go and see them. But you come and see us. Yes; but you insist. Then you like us only as well as you like the Pernes; you like all sorts of people as well perhaps better than you like us. I have nothing to do with anyone. You shall not group me anywhere. I am everywhere. Don't sit there worrying me to death. . . ."

—D.M. Richardson, *Pilgrimage*

Untitled
March 31 – April 1, 1970
[MSS 0587   16   6]

picnic coffee table. "They told me you
look like (~~stocks~~ ??); (an actor) out
here in stock (plays) and ~~there~~ I ~~can~~ see
they are right." (All nicey chatsy.)
        But the coffee is out.
        I go downstairs & out of the building at
the front of which is a very large & old (semi
Spanish deco) kind of converted Writing
Room. A stairway painted orange (dirty),
leading inward. Main room, out, trimmed in
(painted badly) an old & very dirty, shitty
yellow. Walls are of square tiles, piss
(nothing) green. Between back (stair
ivory) & front (door) is a high glass-
plastic wall (easily assailed for those with
good legs) & beneath it, behind it (protecting
it from the front) is an electric train (Dan
Culliton, ala, the thought runs thru my mind
like Dan; at last got house that looks rich
enough; has train; worked hard; why not?;
let him enjoy himself.) Coils of plastic circuits,
gummy joints of precious wire endings:
Some toy production number, incorporated
as perpetual Christmas into the habits
of the house.
        A young (friendly blonde) girl comes
in in white tennis shoes, & white (else),
loaves & gaily (& effortlessly) springs over
white plastic fence (a high tennis-net?)
& goes onto stairs.
        I dash out. The coffee is gone.
Munya, in rush, is outside, far off
from stable, down field, by tubs, washing

Happily,   XV

The literary is a special quirk.
The wall-builder comes to work
and speaks of Hitler and the books he's read.
My next-door neighbor comes instead
and pleads with me I need a woman.
The way is found;
I am too charitable
to give it ground:

a man is woman.
that's a basic fact.
I dig your being here alive...

I lie.

I write. I try
to speak
for the both of us.

I've sworn off honey.
I won't eat sweets.
I meet myself backwards,
an earthworm, head to tail:
parthenogenesis.

I lack balls, you say.
You lie.
I lack my feet.
I birth myself.
Tame python, fed on cotton,
come, with hugs,
to embrace
his charity,
his joyous nemesis.

Untitled
August – December, 1972
[MSS 0587   16   8]

mouse   home
avow   found
               (mies)
field   home
dispel   (leave
               (tree
               (aive
               alive)

1. a (b) c d e
2. a (b) c d e   yipper
3. a b c d e   immaculate
4. a b c (d) e
5. a (b) c d e

5 st: 5 lle.
3 ft: 'absence knive':
alt. stanzas.

                              shown   burnish   gotten
                                                    brittle
hound   gone   weather   burn   earnest   awe
enough   avaunt   (neither)   ↓   Teuton
plow   assault   sauerkraut   mice
         (somersault)   ennoble (sp?)   (without)   Laertes
passion   moon   fuertes
absolute   prime   mourn   appeal   sky
alley   imposter?   (moon)   (remedy)   (disguise)
another   writer   bitter yearn
Adam   height   idea
act   been   Shoulder
graph   'The Dance':   (in)   Soldier
(giraffe) 1.   eyes.   (graph)
                                naive
after

Appropriately,   a
the shot: the aim from the shoulder.   (b)
The tin-'Bang!', and the popcorn   c
Comes prize without the asking.   d
Bright laughter-on-the-rocks.   e

2.

Here, the ferris-wheel: a
A cupie-doll to hold: (b)
a bauble for your awe   c
(and mine): the eyes agape: d
You wonder where you're at.   e

3.

Laughter, laughter, laughter!   a
Across the painted alleys,   b
Blue of sky: Red-violet   c
Canvas. Yellow sun.   d
Hot roasted corn with butter.   e

Untitled
January, 1975 – October, 1976
[MSS 0587   16   9]

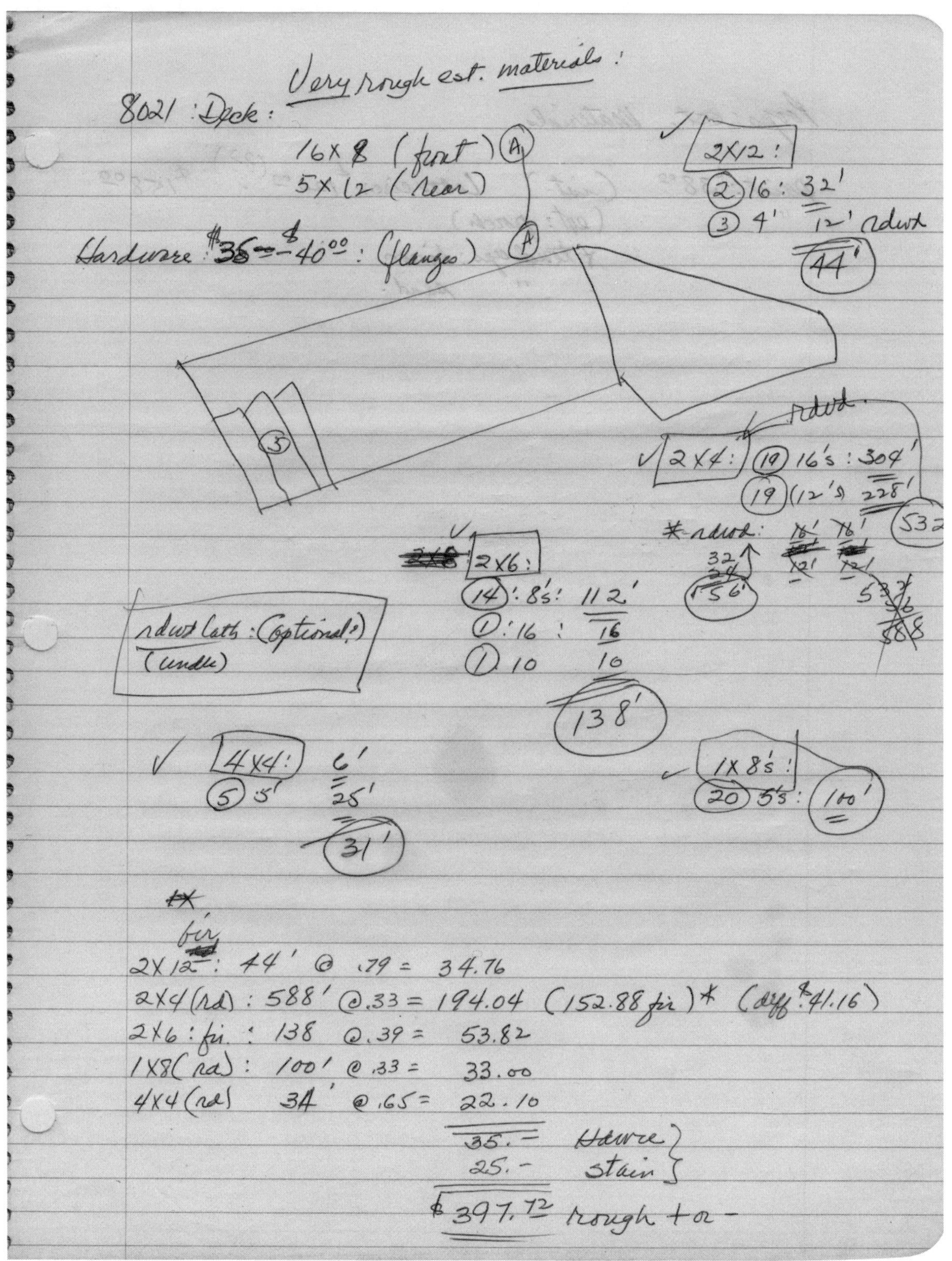

8021 : Deck :

Very rough est. materials :

16 X 8 (front) (A)
5 X 12 (rear)

Hardware : $35⁰⁰ – $40⁰⁰ : (flanges)

(A)

#X
fir
2 X 12 : 44' @ .79 = 34.76
2 X 4 (rd) : 588' @ .33 = 194.04 (152.88 fir) * (diff $41.16)
2 X 6 : fir : 138 @ .39 = 53.82
1 X 8 (rd) : 100' @ .33 = 33.00
4 X 4 (rd) 34' @ .65 = 22.10

35. — Hdwre }
25. — Stain }
$397.⁷² rough + or –

Untitled
June, 1975 – May, 1978
[MSS 0587   17   1]

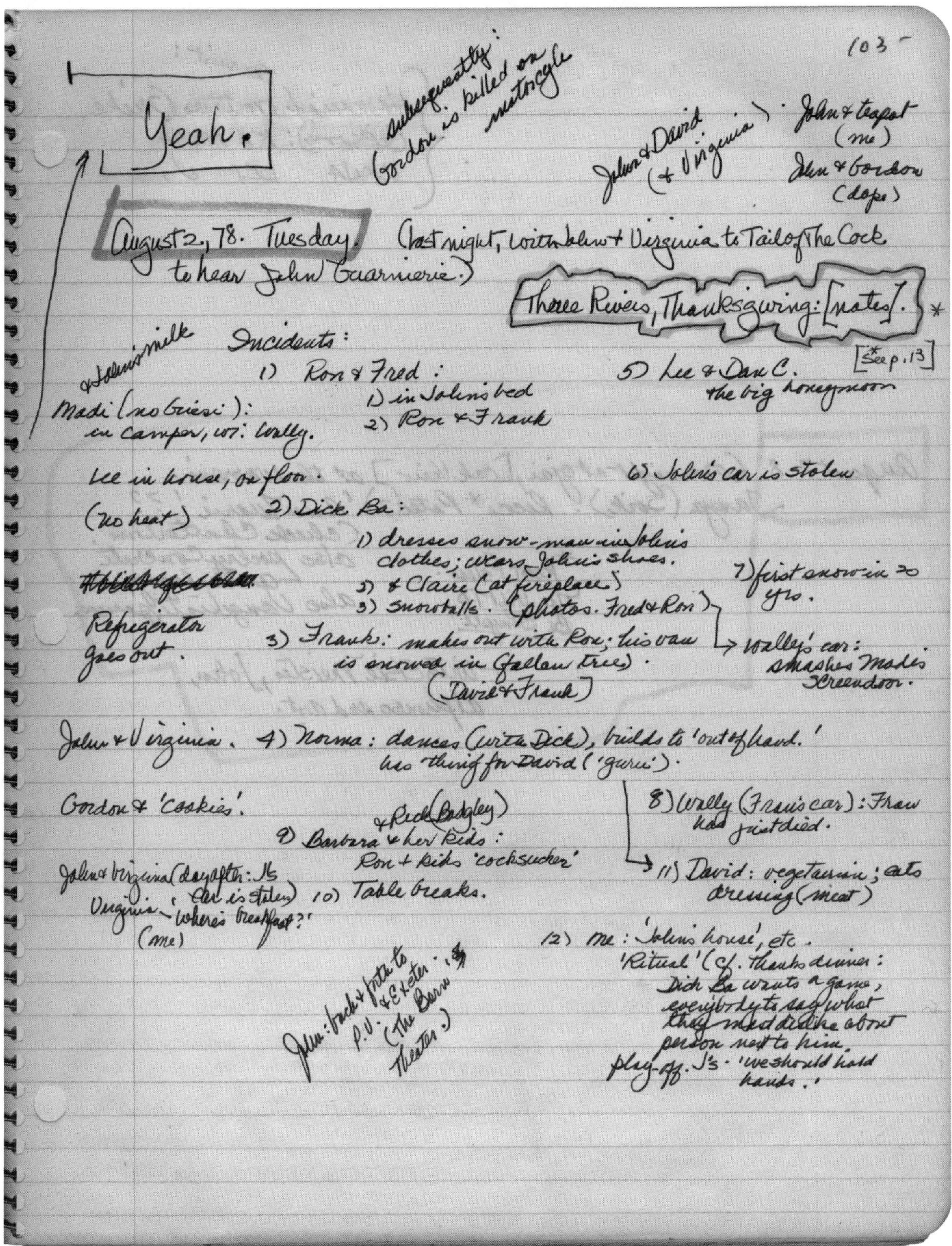

Yeah.

subsequently:
Gordon is killed on
motorcycle

John & David
(+ Virginia)

John & teapot
(me)

John & Gordon
(dope)

August 2, 78. Tuesday   (last night, with John + Virginia to Tail of The Cock
to hear John Guarnieri.)

Three Rivers, Thanksgiving: [notes]. *

[* see p.13]

John's milk

Incidents:

1) Ron & Fred :
   1) in John's bed
   2) Ron & Frank

5) Lee & Dan C.
   the big honeymoon

Madi (no Griesi):
in camper, w: Cally.

Lee in house, on floor.

(no heat)

6) John's car is stolen

2) Dick Ba:
   1) dresses snow-man in John's
      clothes; wears John's shoes.
   3) & Claire (at fireplace)
   3) snowballs. (photos. Fred & Ron)

7) first snow in 20
   yrs.

Refrigerator
goes out.

3) Frank: makes out with Ron; his van
   is snowed in (fallen tree).
   (David & Frank)

wally's car:
smashes Madi's
screendoor.

John & Virginia.   4) Norma: dances (with Dick), builds to 'out of hand.'
                      has thing for David ('guru').

Gordon & 'cookies'.

                      & Rick (Badgley)
   9) Barbara & her kids:
      Ron + kids 'cocksucker'

8) Wally (Frank's car): Frank
   had just died.

John & Virginia (day after: It's
Virginia: car is stolen)
'where's breakfast?'
(me)

10) Table breaks.

11) David: vegetarian; eats
    dressing (meat)

12) me: 'John's house', etc.
    'Ritual' (cf. Thanks dinner:
    Dick Ba writes a game,
    everybody to say what
    they liked/dislike about
    person next to him.
    play-off. J's: 'we should hold
              hands.'

John: back & forth to
P.V. & Exeter:
(The Barn
Theater.)

1/25 Take ride to sunset work from 9:30 – 6:30 Can't understand how I am where I am? I drive around and around in circles. I feel uncomfortable. Ride home with Ronny the black man with the yellow camera and get ride to Canyon Store. Have fish and beans and rice. See Bob who goes crazy!

1/26 Work from 9:30 – 6:30 get ride to Sunset and catch bus get there 5 min late. Have good day work take bus home and eat at "Murders." Walk home get high with Kevin and go to Scot's and meet Mark.

1/27 Work on Aftermath from 10 – 5 in dime. Eat at sj gallat afternoon. Gets cold but beutful day.

1/28 Sleep in till 10:00 decide not to work due to fatigue. Go for hike then walk to thriftys for undies and soap and magazine. Stop at Canyon Store then home to do dishes and make beans + rice for work.

1/29 From 9:30 – 7:00 ride bus there with Bm back. Give Karen some beer.

1/30 9:30 – 6:30 another wet one ride bus both ways.

1/31 9:30 – 6:00 get home just in time to see "Lord of The Rings."

2/1 9:30 – 6:30 get ride to work take bus home. Beutful clouds. Trouble with gaurd at Capitol. Eat great dinner with Bob. Do laundry.

2/2 Work from 8:20 – 6:30 get ride there take bus home. Have big problem trying to cash check. Get twenty from Scot for Aftermath. Eat dinner and take bath.

2/3 Wake at 9:30 feel at home in bed like a child on the weekend home from school. Have been straight so far this month. Facing old self in world I haven't found my place in alone. Have hot cakes for breakfast and hike up hill eating shrooms as I go. Ran into Bob on way down walk to canyon store and back and laugh with Austin + Bob

WIlliam

jAMES

12·15·79

let the ships be quiet.
don't linger here: them
3 part-time soldiers
(lopsided) saluting last taps
recorded atop a carnival van

don't linger
that plastic grass.
can be used again
limp across another hole
               of a gravestone
             we celebrate
good will

And rooms stay rooms
we need to live in.

                    don't linger
        here

At five he said he wd grow up to remember it,
that feeling he had that he wasn't expected to be there
children are not expected to be there they just happen
and he was not really a child, he knew that &
he resolved that one day he wd tell them that
little pitchers have big ears that they are expected
to be seen and not heard was horseshit it was all
horseshit and still is worrying about the telephone bill
(for example) and the latest bank statement
        which is what makes romance
      when there is none and few scientists
around to keep up the description. Stein said that
not me and she's right people don't understand that.

and that grass
when of course I am not
your side the pool table

1

whenever I wanted to make music
there was lights lit in the room
and Santa Claus no kid
would wake up to
            doubtless pissing the bed

One always apologizes for that

        them nagging refrains

    a bag of hardtack
flung dud bullets
thru the door

            not that death was everywhere

hell
you knew that
                (them)
Christmas celebrations

a longhoul to brass valley
where I buried her

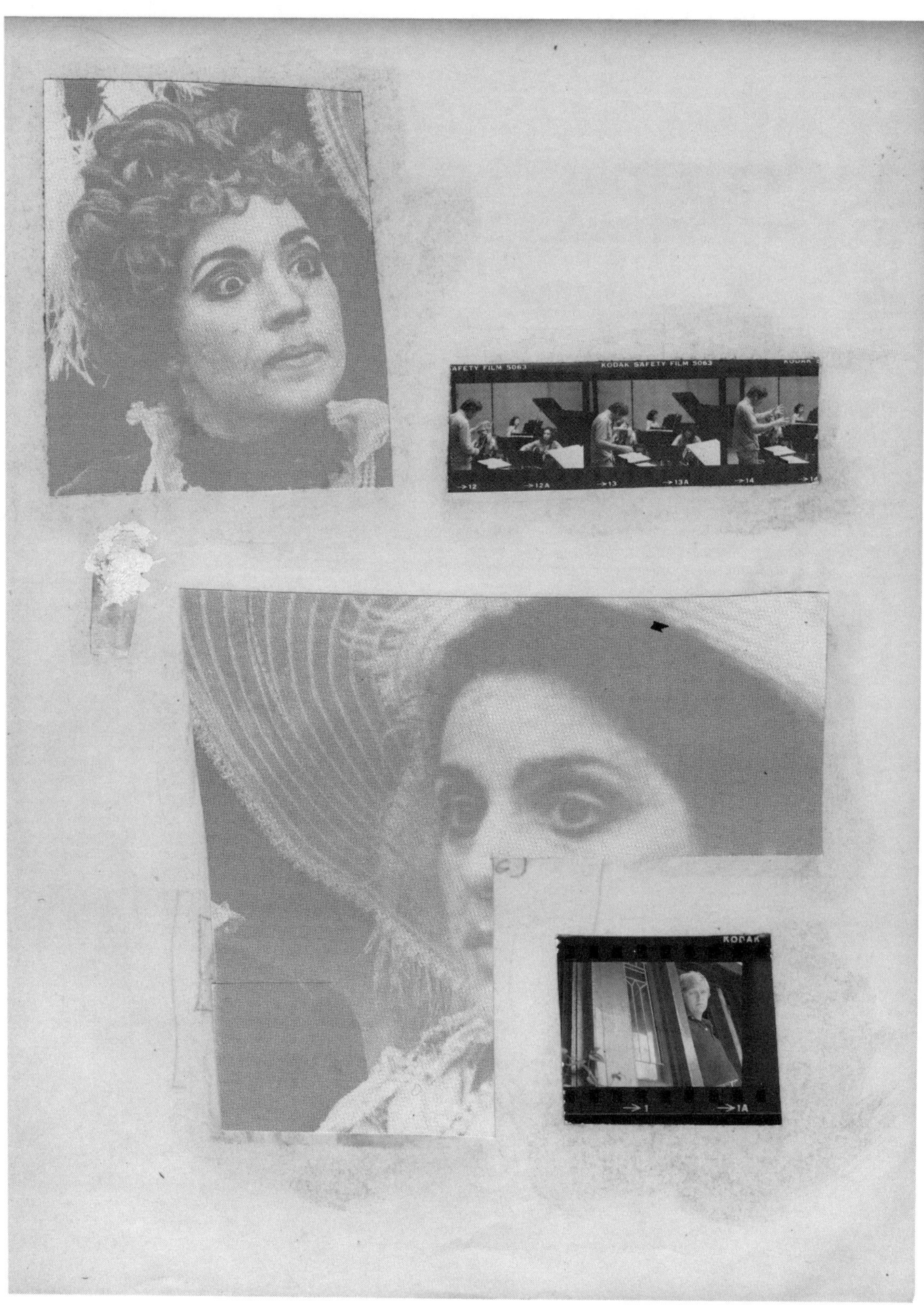

Tuesday Night
July, 1980 – September, 1981
[MSS 0587   17   6]

— — — ;

pg. 2:
Goodbye.

Standford Drew was his name a great
ot of a lad graduated @ millionaire
and bougat Cuba for 2 gallons eggshell
and a qt of navajo white

Surmise.
blinding sun and flies
in droves.

Eat Chicken
1980 – 1982
[MSS 0587   17   7]

"What is mine is not everybodys," sd the Lady.

snow it
snowed 20 years in one
night that everyone hell kiva

Rain telephones, addresses & hangs up.
Tales no finger can lay hand to. Them
days was them days, worrisome ironies
piers plowed chicken coops.

Rangers rode the peach trees

then.

One night, modelling,
        a tiger-girl
             in suit
    Jack takes pictures
        with his color poloroid.

                        'Denny's
                         Special'

and.
    and.   (I have not
            gone back.)

disastrous.
        that

her me wheel chair
has to be lifted out of bed.
She wanted me to come
be with her, I was ready
to go. Helen wrote she was
moving to 3 rooms. Ilene crying
said Grace's hip was on the
around in 3 days. Grace was
getting childish I knew little
than that she did not want
me to come. She didn't

move. Her & Roy went to the cabin in
Mts a wk last wk. Make sure Grace went
to Bob's as they would not release her
if no one was home. I'll sure tell her
about lot of things. I'll go later if
Grace is able & wants to I'll bring her
here. Helen Roan took inward hemorrages
yesterday they operated on her right
away. Don't know full particulars. Ed's
working at Riverside gets most everyday in.
Grace got your card said she had a good
laugh about it. & tell you thanks. Bout
all for now. Hon let you know when I hear
any more. Come over soon again know better
ask you to (write) Love Mom.
Grace address
2/0 311 W. Pike
Houston.

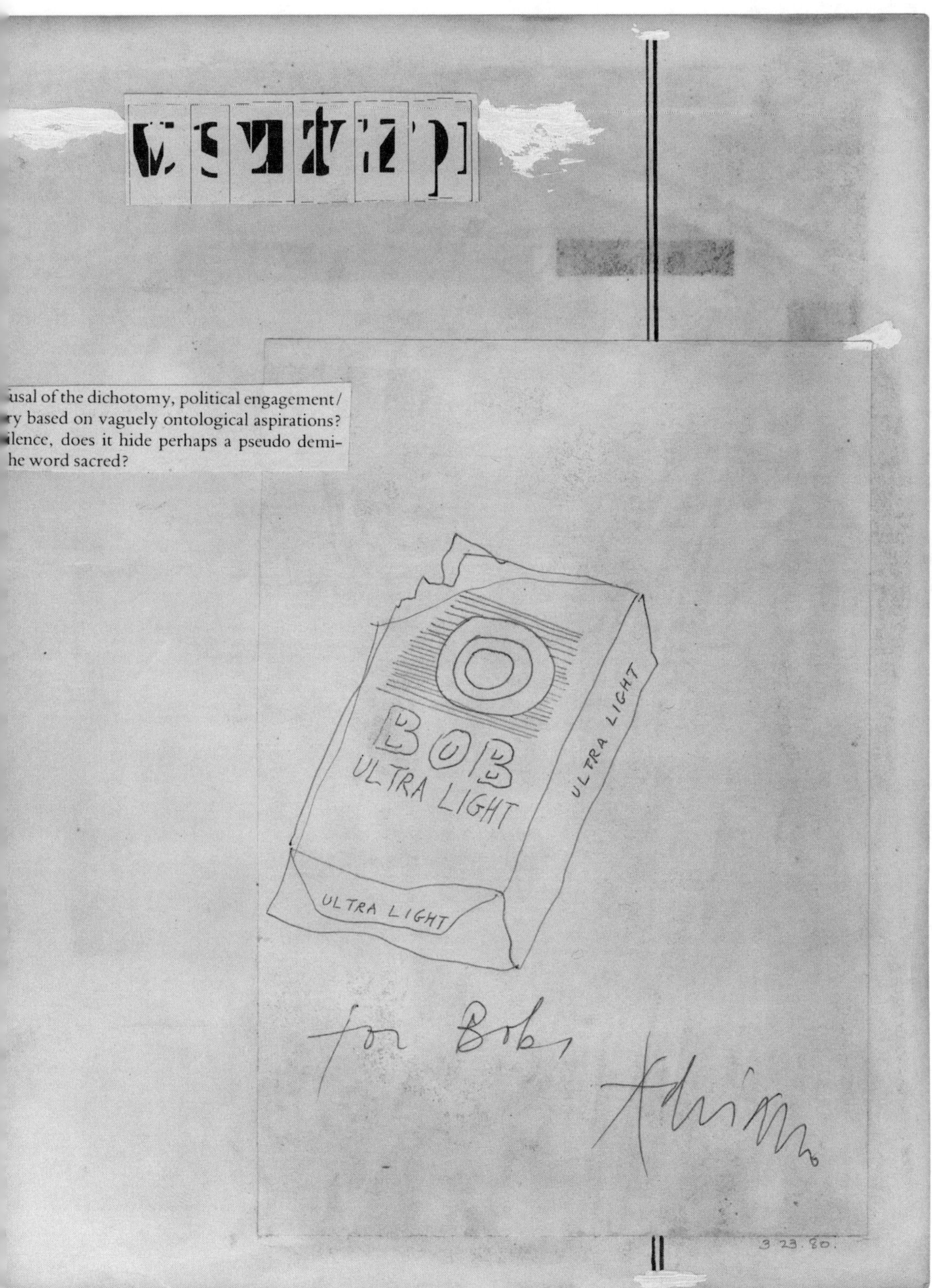

usal of the dichotomy, political engagement/
ry based on vaguely ontological aspirations?
lence, does it hide perhaps a pseudo demi-
he word sacred?

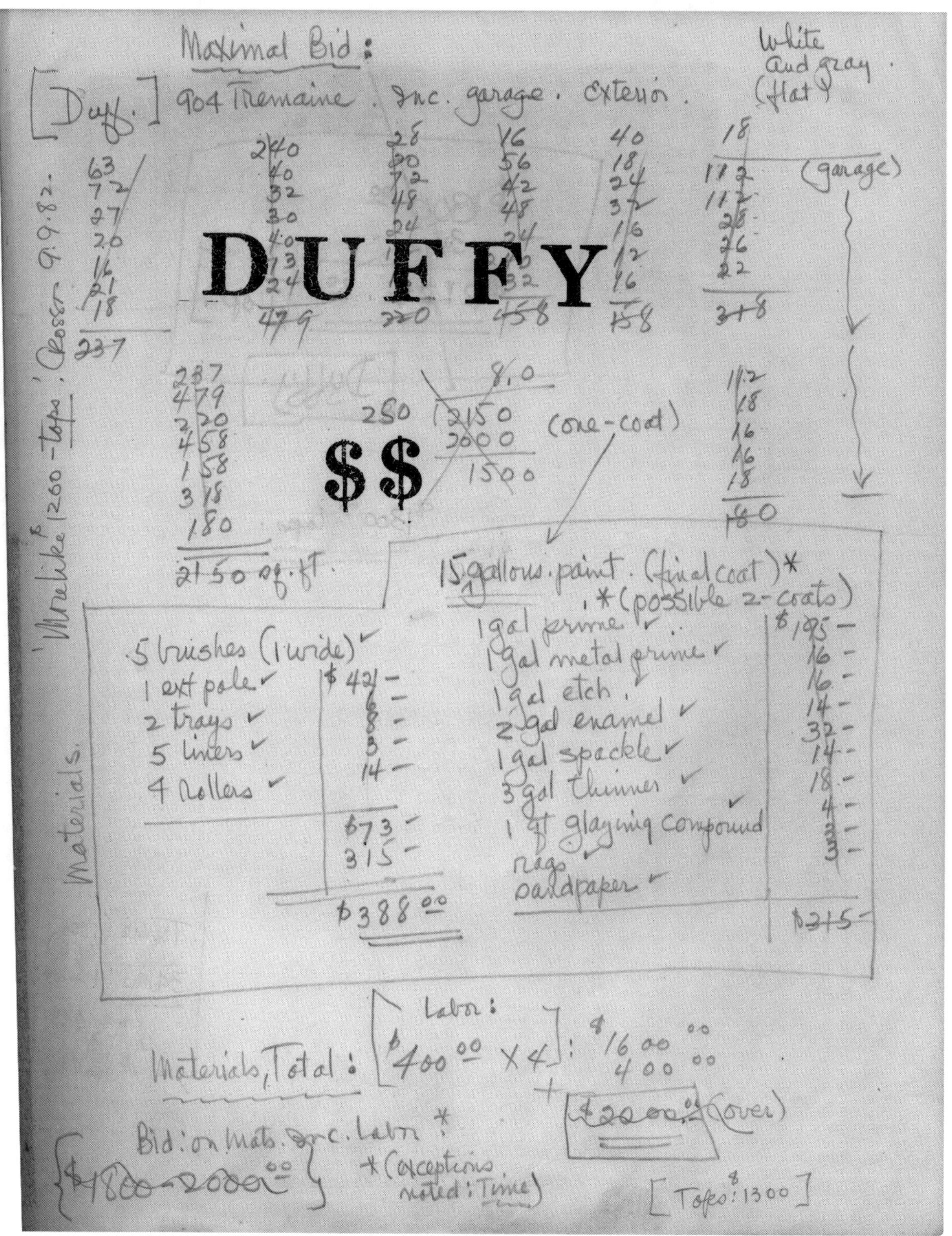

Maximal Bid:

White
and gray.
(flat)

[Duff.] 904 Tremaine . Inc. garage . Exterior .

(garage)

63	240	28	16	40	18
7 2	40	20	56	18	
27	32	72	42	24	11 2
20	30	48	48	32	11 2
16	40	64	24	16	28
21	13	48	32	12	76
18	24			16	22
237	479	220	458	158	318

'Murelike 1260 - Tape . Closer 9.9.82.

Materials.

237		8 0		11 2
479	250	2150		18
320		2000	(one-coat)	16
458		1500		16
158				18
318				180
180				

2150 sq. ft.

5 brushes (1 wide)
1 ext pole $ 42 —
2 trays   8 —
5 liners   3 —
4 Rollers   14 —

                     673 —
                     315 —

                   $ 388 00

15 gallons. paint. (final coat) *
          . * (possible 2-coats)

1 gal prime . $ 195 —
1 gal metal prime   16 —
1 gal etch .   16 —
2 gal enamel   14 —
1 gal spackle   32 —
3 gal thinner   14 —
1 qt glazing compound   18 —
rags   4 —
sandpaper   3 —

                       $ 215

Labor:
Materials, Total :   [$ 400 00 X 4] : $ 16 00 00
                                            4 00 00
                                         +
                                         $ 20 00 00 (over)

Bid : on Mats. Inc. Labr *
{ $ 1800 - 2000 00 }   * (exceptions,
                         noted : Time)   [Total : 1300]

2

(pause)

SPEAKER:

Monday 12-13-71

Dear Bob —
    Where are you? And how are you?
Please dash off a line and let
me know if you can. Don't want
to lose you!
               Much love,
                  June

P.S. Scratched note onto Wally's card to say I've not
been back to California coming here to 68 — but
you know, don't know if he'll even remember me! (Hope you do!)
And I hope you are well + happy. Love - J - (over)

Armond is looking into jobs with small publishers of art
education materials in Massachusetts now. Has become
disgruntled at McGraw-Hill.
    I am not doing anything — not even pacing my cage any-
more. Just take to my bed with a sleeping pill and those [illegible].
    I'll [illegible] (back home [illegible] place in San [illegible])
Don't know how to fight or start over this time — looks gone + health ruined. (No longer
go to bed for anything but sleep.)
By the way, I never did thank you for that lovely week
(or was it two?) you gave me in Los Angeles, when I stayed with you on
vacation. It was heaven and you were beautiful and much too
generous. I'll always remember it.
    Kampe (still flying; sold his drilling rig) has been going with a (slightly older) married woman for several years.
As of last month she is divorced + has rather sizable alimony; don't guess they
can afford to marry + lose it. She's used to a good income! (I knew Kampe's
[illegible] her agate best much better than mother's
and so is his friendship.) He's been collecting material to build himself a
small, fast plane. Still working on [illegible] (a little [illegible] readymade [illegible] be much cheaper.) »

→ He's also taken up soaring (or glider-ing). Didn't know he was interested.
And Armond has begun playing tennis again — indoors here. Bob misses being able
to paint weekends. [We live in a SMALL but still expensive - studio apt.] And you? but no bed! Love - June

errant pulstate~~~~ autiation of what I must abhor~.
Having spent, then, that devil in myself. °Cease
the lie.

How, then, would I be different?

ANSWERS:
THE ANTIPHONAL

OPEN. (BREAKFAST SPECIAL: THRIFTY DRUG)

'AC-DC!' had the heart erected,
the morning-hots on all sides.

Until I asked the waitress,
Elly, what it meant: 'AC-BC,'
Elly said, 'American cheese
with buttered crusts.'

    Shit, I sighed.

the answers always come
in simple sandwiches.

PROLOGUE.

why do you come home with me?
don't you see how I am
taut as a rusted clavier
string? I do

    not need
    sounding:

the music you want
needs more ceremony
& more silence
than I am
used to.

Up to noon they fell in sleeping
grass (or the great dread wagon
some groaning brought) and lay
teeth topmost; toasting
omelettes & crusts of holy brail
the way tall riders did once
before the philistines had come.
Upwards they went, the likes of
witches, stoned to the mountains
and wound their locks in groins
of labor, hard as rocks.

Time sends sales popping.
The ones with comics in their
lockets gave last night to
whomsoever. With wet, blond
kisses they stole love's labor
& rode off with some
applause.

Stakes
July–October, 1983
[MSS 0587 18 4]

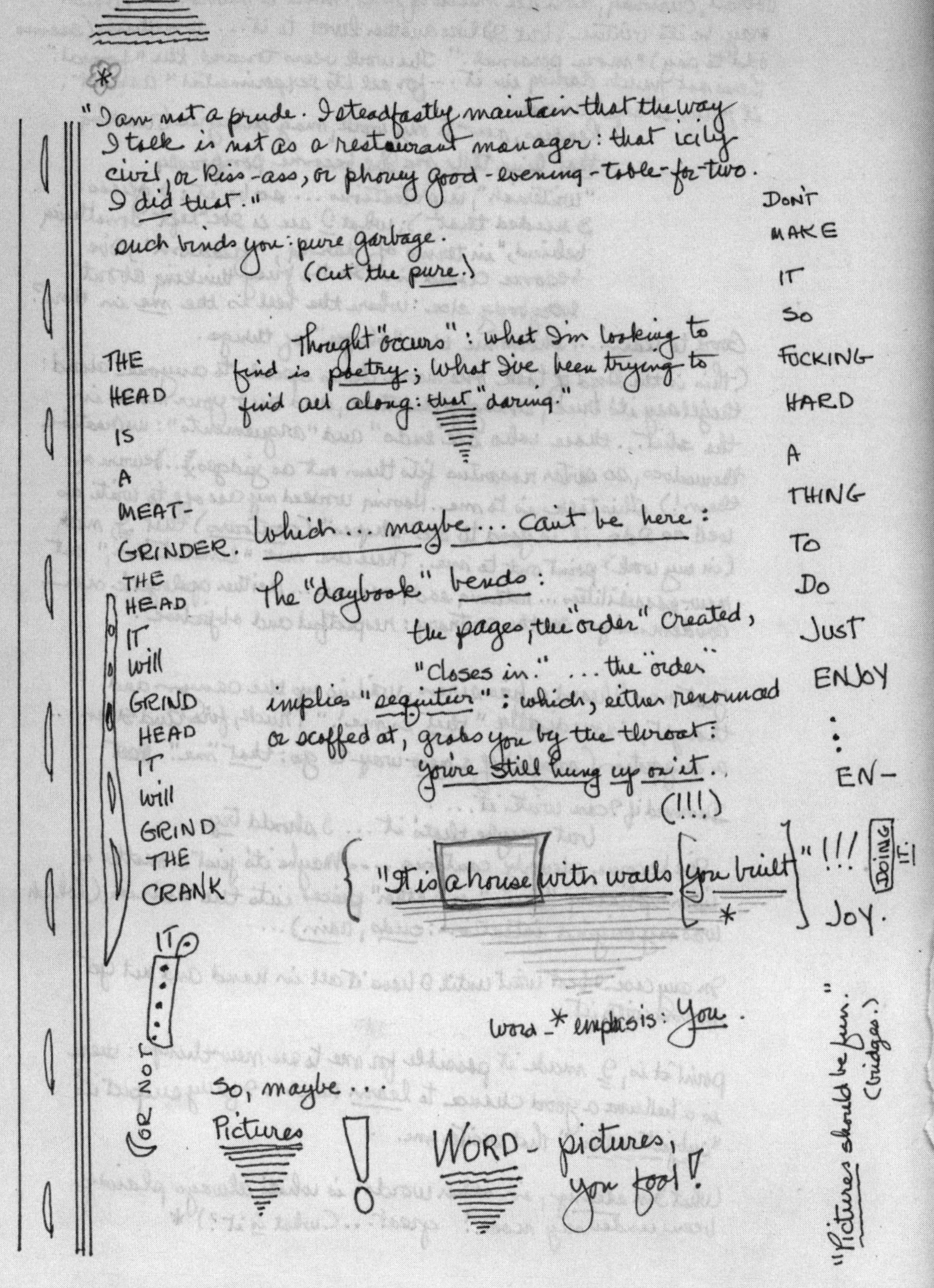

"I am not a prude. I steadfastly maintain that the way
I talk is not as a restaurant manager: that icily
civil, or Kiss-ass, or phoney good-evening-table-for-two.
I did that."

such binds you: pure garbage.
(Cut the pure.)

THE
HEAD
IS
A
MEAT-
GRINDER.
THE
HEAD
IT.
WILL
GRIND
HEAD
IT.
WILL
GRIND
THE
CRANK
IT
(OR NOT)

Thought "occurs": what I'm looking to
find is poetry; what I've been trying to
find all along: that "daring."

Which ... maybe ... can't be here:

The "daybook" bends:
the pages, the "order" Created,
"Closes in." ... the "order"
implies "sequitur": which, either renounced
or scoffed at, grabs you by the throat:
you're still hung up on it.
(!!!)

{ "It is a house with walls you built" !!!
* } JOY.

DOING IT.

DON'T
MAKE
IT
SO
FUCKING
HARD
A
THING
TO
DO
JUST
ENJOY
...
EN-
JOY.

word -* emphasis: You.

So, maybe ...
Pictures

WORD - pictures,
you fool!

"Pictures should be fun."
(bridges.)

ADVENT_s

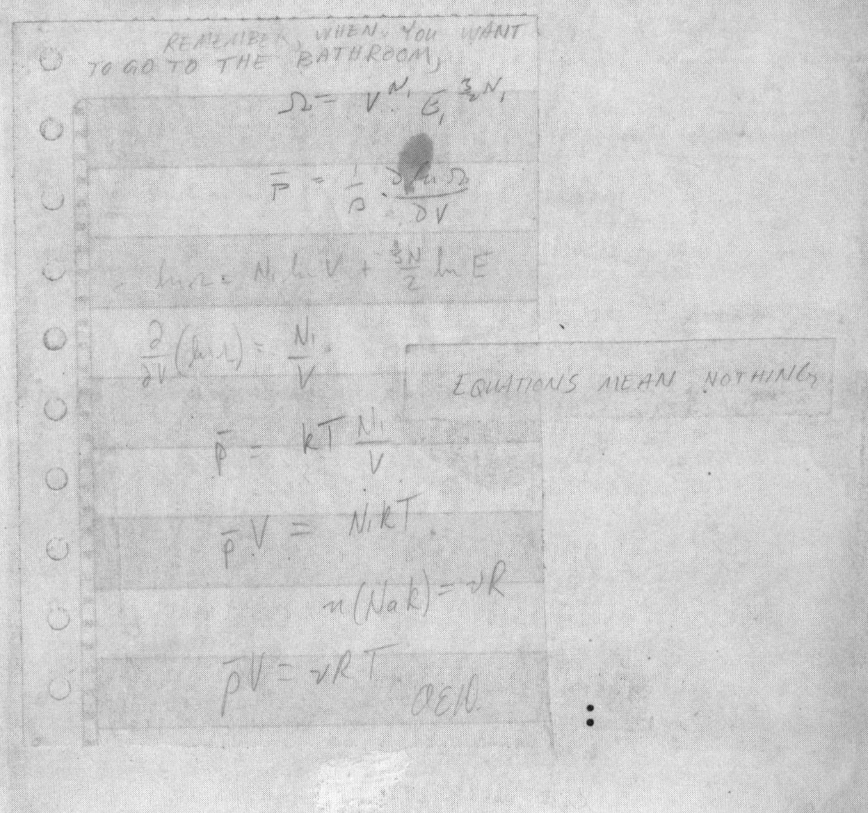

OF

PASCAL

Untitled
February – June, 1984
[MSS 0587   19   2]

3:30.

lesson drives off.... comes back.

*

And when people sell the house, they leave it...
Tempered rooms.
a sprig of ivy, growing through a crack in the fireplace.

— my coat-lining . . .
        silk, I guess.

                fine sleeve.

My favorite coat.
(fallen to bits, but
        still me.)

        [have to pace] pierce my armpits.

    pretty cloth.
    Fine coat.

2.22:
[Have done up] NEA application, ready to mail.
        Pleased, this time . . . used 20 pp.
        [tight] work.
        (we'll see).

[opera bores me.]

        re-read [neuhaus letter] ten times.*
                    (*over) →
                    stay up.

```
char _Wicat_Version_[] =
static   char *sccsid = "(
/*
 * lpf -- Line printer f:
 */


#include <stdio.h>
#include <sgtty.h>
#include <signal.h>

#define LINELN   240   /*r(
#define PAGELN   66
#define EJLINE   10000000
#define SKPLINE 0

int       anydone;
char      linebuf[LINELN+2:
int       ov;
char      ovbuf[LINELN];
FILE      *in      = {stdin:
FILE      *out;
char      *ban="\0";
int       npages  = 1;
char      chrtab[][16];
int       lineno;
struct    sgttyb ttyb = { !
struct    tchars ttyc = { -
char      obuf[BUFSIZ];
int       onemt();
char      *middle="\0";   /:
int       transparent=0;    .
char      c;

main(argc, argv)
char **argv;
{

        if ((out = fopen
                fprintf(
                exit(1);
        }
        setbuf(out, obuf:
        stty(fileno(out).
        ioctl(fileno(out:
        signal(SIGEMT, o:
        argv++;   /*point
        argc--;
        while(**argv ==
                c=argv[0
                switch (
```

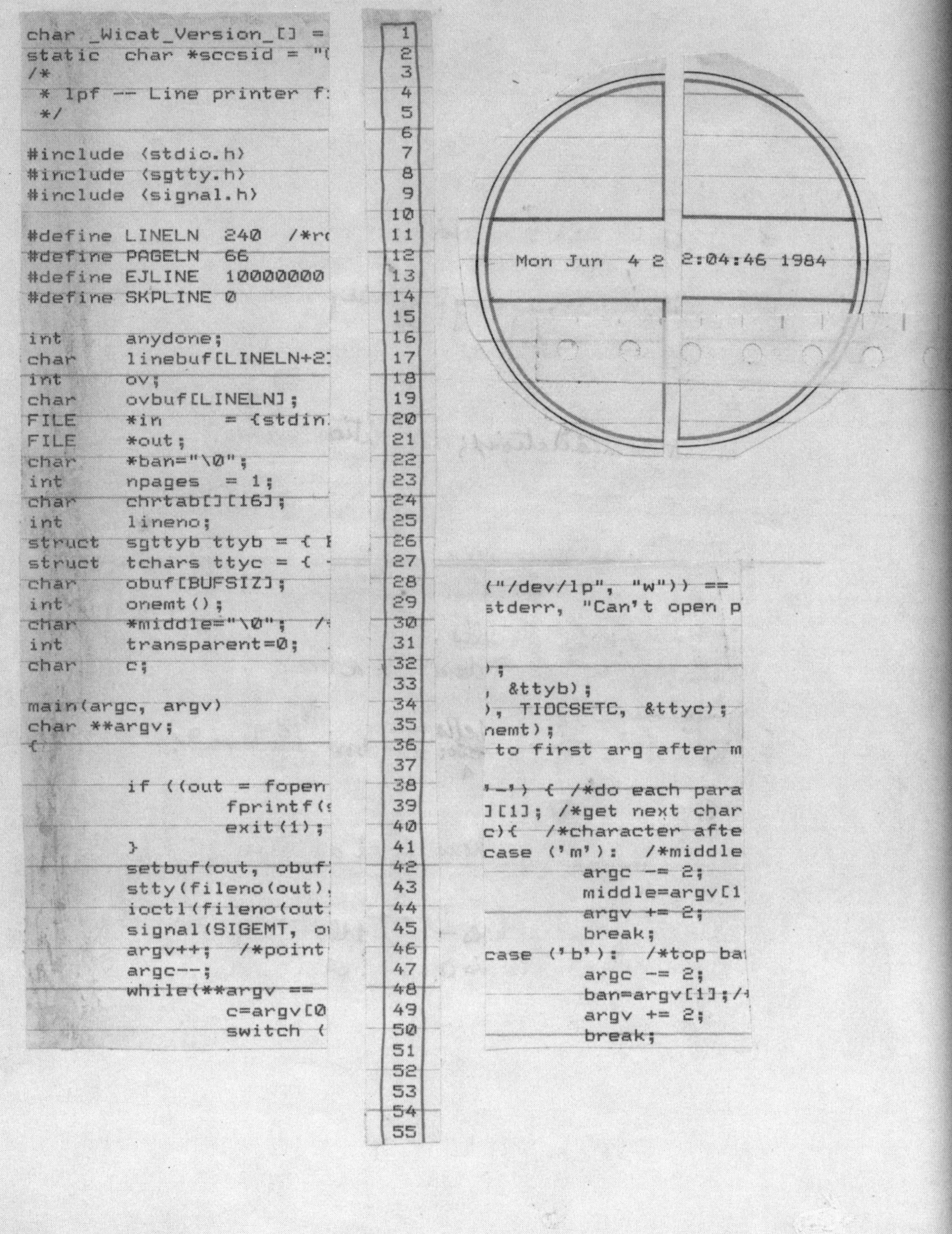


```
("/dev/lp", "w")) ==
stderr, "Can't open p


);
, &ttyb);
), TIOCSETC, &ttyc);
nemt);
 to first arg after m

'-') { /*do each para
][1]; /*get next char
c){   /*character afte
case ('m'):   /*middle
        argc -= 2;
        middle=argv[1
        argv += 2;
        break;
case ('b'):   /*top ba:
        argc -= 2;
        ban=argv[1];/:
        argv += 2;
        break;
```

Moon Soup
August, 1984 – March, 1985
[MSS 0587   19   4]

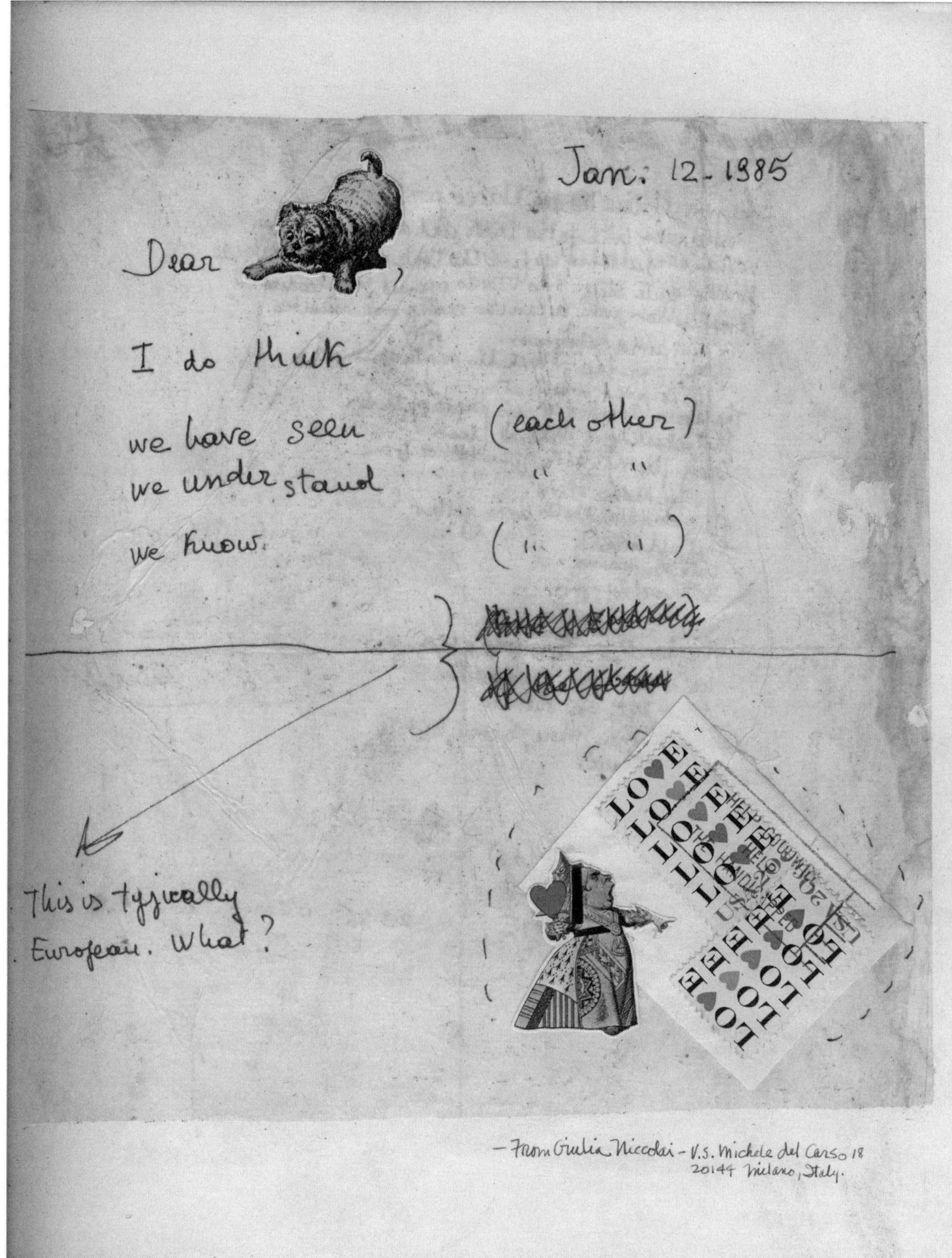

— From Giulia Niccolai – V.S. Michele del Carso 18
20144 Milano, Italy.

Rocks and Cabbages
March – June, 1985
[MSS 0587   20   1]

4.17.85 (Wednesday)

Ann Nitski is right: I am full of shit. There are days I don't believe one word I've written here. I am a mean man, an unhappy man, worried, preposterous to others; arrogant, supercilious, generous for the wrong reasons, at heart unkind.. Bitchy, arch, cruel. Pretentious and lazy: Unenterprising, fretful, cowardly, deceitful — grudging, envious, glib, purposely shallow; an emotional retard, expecting all things delivered on a platter (angry, duplicitous when not), overtalkative, vapid, loud, petty, suspicious, conniving, pompous — given to false flattery and the easy way out. Frightened and false (even to myself): a poseur; harshly self-centered in the eyes of love and friendship; calculating; a squanderer of resource and time. Redundant and vain. Cursed by a sense of humor; sustained by a mistrust of adjectives:
"in love with 'writing' (persistently courting it),
pedantic — blithe in the face of most criticism:
For a fact, overweight (fat),
and not young.

*

Yesterday, driving behind a car that bore the license-plate
TO 1-EGY,
I came home determined to write one (elegy).
I have not.

(Dr. Bob has changed our morning appointment to 1³⁰ pm.)

*

Christine maintains that my sense of humor is satanic.
She (also) may be right.
        This is certainly no novel, here.
    No play.

. . .

        more (daytime) portrait of a man
        scratching his skin off.

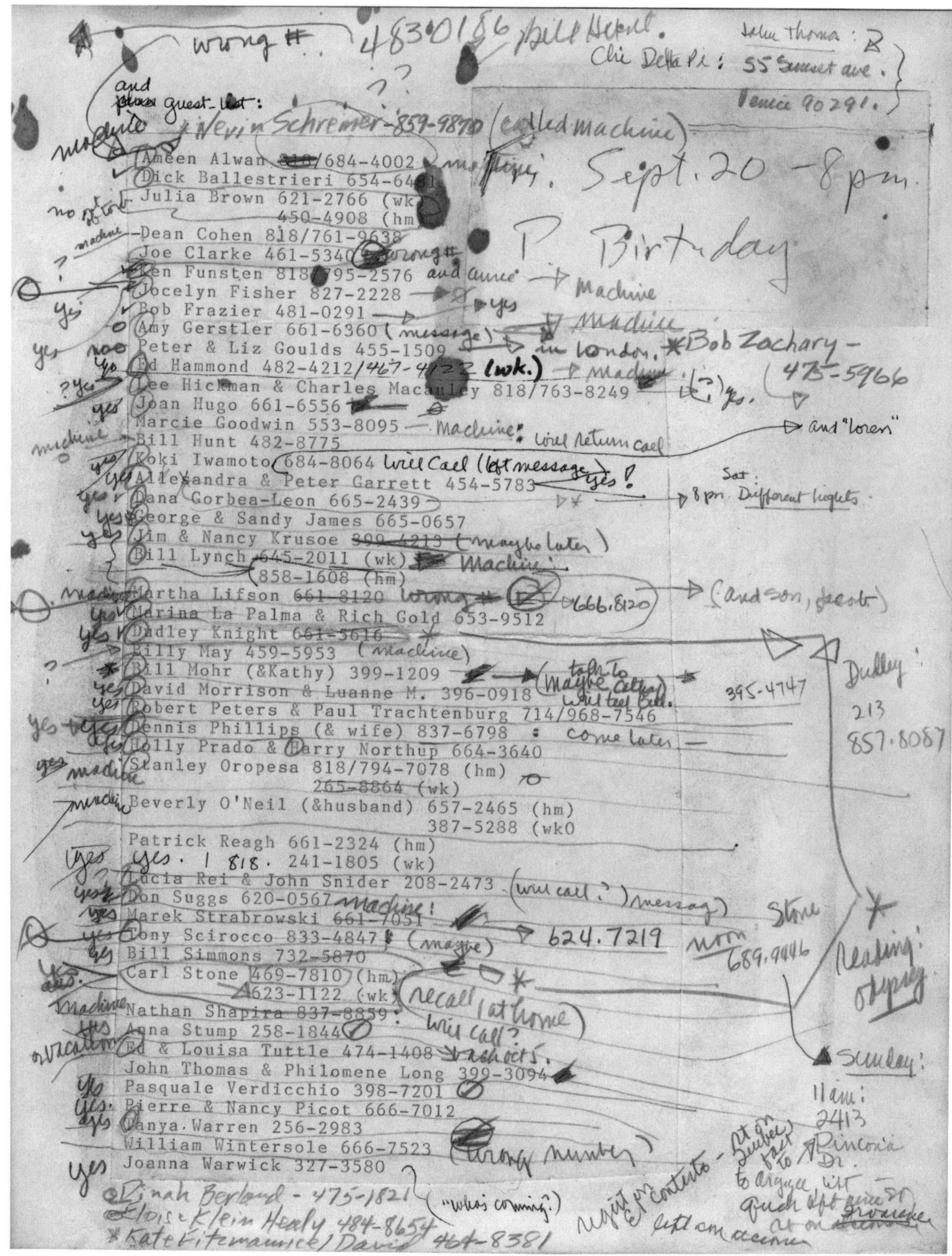

I say that.

Got my new toolbox.
Got tools in order.

Wary,
of the idea.

But Will (WILL)
(do.

OCCIDENTAL COLLEGE
LOS ANGELES • CALIFORNIA 90041

Comparative Literature

Bob Crosson
8021 Jov
L.A. C
900

Poems about Los
Angeles and other
exotic places such
as Sandusky, Ohio,
poetry reading by
Martha Ronk Lifson
at Beyond Baroque
with Don Byrd on
November 15 at
8:30 p.m.
681 Venice Blvd.
Venice, CA.

Rain
December, 1985 – March, 1986
[MSS 0587   20   4]

13ᵗʰ / 5 pm.

Paul phones: says Thomas and Philomine spent last nights
    in a motel: out of van — John not having
    to sleep in his (new) sleeping bag ...

" : what to do?"

    I said pay.

———————————————

(Yesterday, lunch at George's. *
    Day before (Wednesday): meet John and Philomine
    at Bank — Cash: reader's check (in my name)
    and convivial greetings.
                                    * pioneer chicken.

———————————————

14ᵗʰ (2/am):
With Paul to Beyond Baroque: "language poets", (Leland
Hickman) and (prime Herald) Barrett Watten; an
audience of eight (paid) including us, Haley, Harry,
Bill Mohr and others.

*

lessons earned:
    1) ego corrupts
    2) self-indulgence obliterates
    3) "causes" mesmerize
    4) our Muse deserves, if not worship,
        at least more deligent respect.

    5) I am a snob,
    6) without apology.

    7) God needs our help.
    8) Silence is golden.

        9) winter is upon us.

A Sore Foot
March – June, 1986
[MSS 0587   21   1]

establishing schools of thought.
                substantial priority.

____

            i am mad i think i am quite mad
            the way the quakers said it

            with good humor / hard come by, some days.

                the way you don't have enough
                reference books.

            to sharpen.

            (example.

                                    (being an actor maybe.

                                    pagliacci.

                                    shakespeare's fool.

                                            an arrogant,
                                                mean fat prick.

                                        like a Falstaff.

Inauguration
June – August, 1986
[MSS 0587   21   2]

7/23/86

Dear Robt.:

      I've been too much in motion to
stay still long enough to write you that letter
explaining my intentions in regard to your
book. The main point was going to be that if
someone else will do _a_ book by you--if their
destiny is so fortunate--then who am I to stand
in their way. I think ours is one of the few
worlds left in which competition doesn't have
a place! But it might be well to let someone
else publish a different book by you, if there
is one, since we already know I'd do the Day
Book.
      But schedule-wise, in order to do right
by the (14 or so) other books on our stove,
yours wouldn't be able to be served up to the
public until around this time _next_ year. So
you be the judge.
      Let me know, and also about how you are.

Best,

ILLUMINATI
P. O. BOX 67E07
LOS ANGELES, CA 90067

2031

July 23 1986   90-1261/1222

PAY TO THE ORDER OF____ Robert Crosson*********************** | $100.00****

___One Hundred *************************************____ DOLLARS

Santa Monica Bank
33RD STREET AND PICO BOULEVARD
Santa Monica, Calif. 90405

MEMO____ "Daybook" advance roy.

⑇1222126⑇⑇:2031⑈04 050 509⑈⑈

—Schneider—

*

Some of them try to escape crossing the freeway:
Smacked flat and left poem to somebody's father.

others (gang-leaders) go back East to Detroit or somewhere.
to learn test-art of graffitti: and paint murals on any
walls left standing.

*

"a parasite on the State" bit
my lady's breast.
again. under the Harbor freeway:

*

"some of the better ones
are downtown."

*

Rabbits, I say, do not wear hats
(this has been said before). If you see
a photograph of one (portly) wearing
a sombrero, in robes, sash, or yellow
overalls, watch out. Rabbits don't wear
beards usually: I have never known one
with one. and tend to mistrust show
of jewelry.

They tend to drink and smoke.
and marry often.

*)

Rattods either.

— Crosson /
/ 10am.

The Establishment
October, 1986 – February, 1987
[MSS 0587   21   4]

VIRGIL THOMSON

222 WEST 23rd STREET
NEW YORK 11, N. Y.

14 January 1987

Dear Mr. Crosson,

All thanks for your handsome <u>Geographies</u>, also
for the excerpts about me and Gertrude Stein from
your <u>Daybooks</u>.

The latter goes in the archive as 'About 4 Saints'.

All good wishes to you and your work,

      Very sincerely,

      Virgil Thomson

      Virgil Thomson

Robert L. Crosson
8021 Jovenita Canyon Road
Los Angeles, California   90046

lr

Mr. Jack Miles: april 14. 87.

Re. your Pronouncement (Endpapers: BOOK REVIEW, Sunday
April 12): that Poetry, and books of, will no longer,
regularly, be reviewed. Instead, regularly, a poem:
to be published every Sunday.

Your inclusion--obviously the first-installment--of
William Matthews' witty and urbane poem, SEARCH FOR
THE PERFECT PASTA, would underline, however subliminally,
our dilemma. . .

Few people read poetry, that's a fact: it does not sell
newspapers. That there is a division among poets and
Schools of poetry is also a fact. The best that an editor
can do, perhaps, is SEARCH FOR THE PERFECT PASTA.
 I strenuously disagree.

I am a poet.
One-poem-a-week doesn't address the issue: that we are
alive and well and very much a part of our City.
Your plausible and good argument would mark the Death
of poetry. Anywhere. . .

Alas, pedestrian argument.
A contemporary fact.
To be lamented.

Sincerely,

(yours)

Robert L. Crosson

Robert Crosson
8021 Jovenita Canyon Rd.
Los Angeles, CA. 90046

(213) 654-6527

Audience
May – July, 1987
[MSS 0587   22   2]

Chapter II
Casey at the Bat

I never got to know him, except the sodas he doled out,
free: to keep fast kids from sweating.

(you don't wear rotten tennis-shoes to church.)

The Maxim is what you hit fast,
and start running. It is what, Sundays,
congregate.

tin pail-fulls of sand
and a miniature shovel.

Chapter III
Target

stepped over a doorsill. affixing
another room. or a second place
to be entered.

by accident.

He was plainly there for business,
not charity.

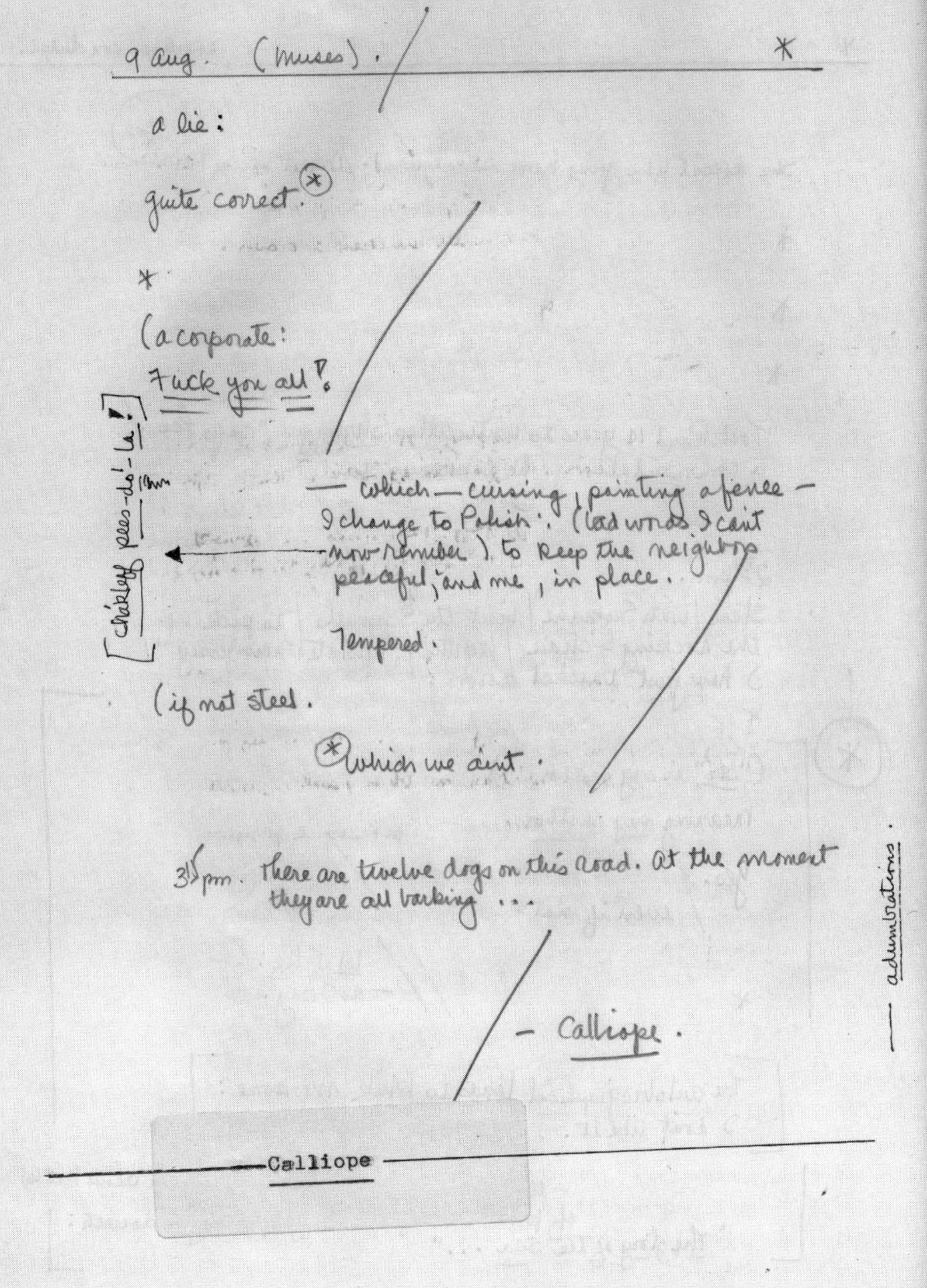

9 aug. (muses). /   *

a lie:

quite correct. ⊛

*

(a corporate:
Fuck you all !.

[chablof pees-di-la!]   12mm

— which — cursing, painting a fence —
I change to Polish: (bad words I can't
now remember) to keep the neighbors
peaceful, and me, in place.

Tempered.

(if not steel.

⊛ Which we aint.

3.15pm. There are twelve dogs on this road. At the moment
they are all barking ...

— Calliope.

— adumbrations.

Calliope

Untitled
September – November, 1987
[MSS 0587   22   4]

[Number Three]

1

all
~~Everything~~ is edge
~~granted~~ ('endless')
Depths,
upon which decay
clings like mould.

I shudder.

In the mind,
envisioned eyelashes,
all-white;
and before the eyes,
unkingly Purple.

In other places,
~~to hear~~ one hears
a song without music.

(Two:)

plateau.
brink, brim, crest, rim
margin, ledge,
border, lip,

[   ]

appearing, seem,
apparition

region, tract of country,
neighborhood, region,

2

all
~~Everything~~ is edge
despite ('endless')
~~Abyss,~~ *Depths,* (abyss)
upon which decay
clings like mould.

I shudder.

In the mind,
ghostly eyelashes,
all-white;
before the eyes,
unkingly Purple.

In ~~exile,~~ *the country*
~~hearing,~~ one hears
a song without tone.

Untitled
November, 1987 – May, 1988
[MSS 0587   23   1]

I don't go around screaming about it.

I mean this.

I am cursed to the Narrative.
The fiction
surrogate

of what isn't there.

Poetry evades

Nemo
May – August, 1988
[MSS 0587   23   2]

following pages: *Untitled*
August – October, 1988
[MSS 0587   23   3]

chez Nemo

You are cordially invited to a feast
to benefit the publication of Robert
Crosson's new volume of poetry,
Daybook.   All subscriptions are tax deductible
and should be made out to:
Isthmus Poetry Foundation / Red Hill Press
[ISTHMUS]

Menu, Sunday, June 5, 12:30 pm

antipasto: Panzanella (Tuscan bread salad)
minestre: Penne con cozze &
(pastas)   Penne alla rabbiata
entrée: Pollo affinnochiato (fenneled chicken)
contorni: Insalata & verdure (salad + vegetables)
dolce: Torta di ricotta (ricotta 'forte')
Caffe, Assorted wines
and apperitifs

subscriptions are $50°° per
person. Please RSVP by
May 30 to (213) 654-6527.

this Feast is sponsored by Nemo's Angels, and
will be held at 3132 Berkeley Circle, Los Angeles.!

[Riverside :]   / HOUSE . .. / 10. 88.

[moulds] : book case.   / hi — 6' lengths
                                 wide — 8' .
face/molds: depth — 7" with m
(top) "round" (edge) : ½"   ① 10'   8¾
                                 plus :
   × ¾   ④ sh
(slope + ⅜ beads) ③   ① top 1⅝"
              plus (under):

¾ × ¾
       ① 10'   1 2 3   exact ht 49¾"
                    ½" × 1" :
   #   (slope : flat round)
  (½ × 3)   11¼"
   2   4   total width
                 ③ 3/4" trim
plus base (from molds)
         ① 10'   ▵ plus 2. "dividers" ¾ each, 8
                        (8½)"   height : ge
                                    ② 6
         [scribbled crossed out]   Shelf facing : ¾ :
                                        ③ 65   (4 beads)
          × ½ × ½" :   ④ 65
                                    1 [side-mount] : 3 sides
                                   (1¼)" : same as)
base mold :   × 14 8 ft
5¼" ≤ (total : ht) :   # these overlap
   ① (front) base 2½" high :   / back base : (5¼) : × ¾" :
          × 1½"   = ① 10' / or ② 10'5

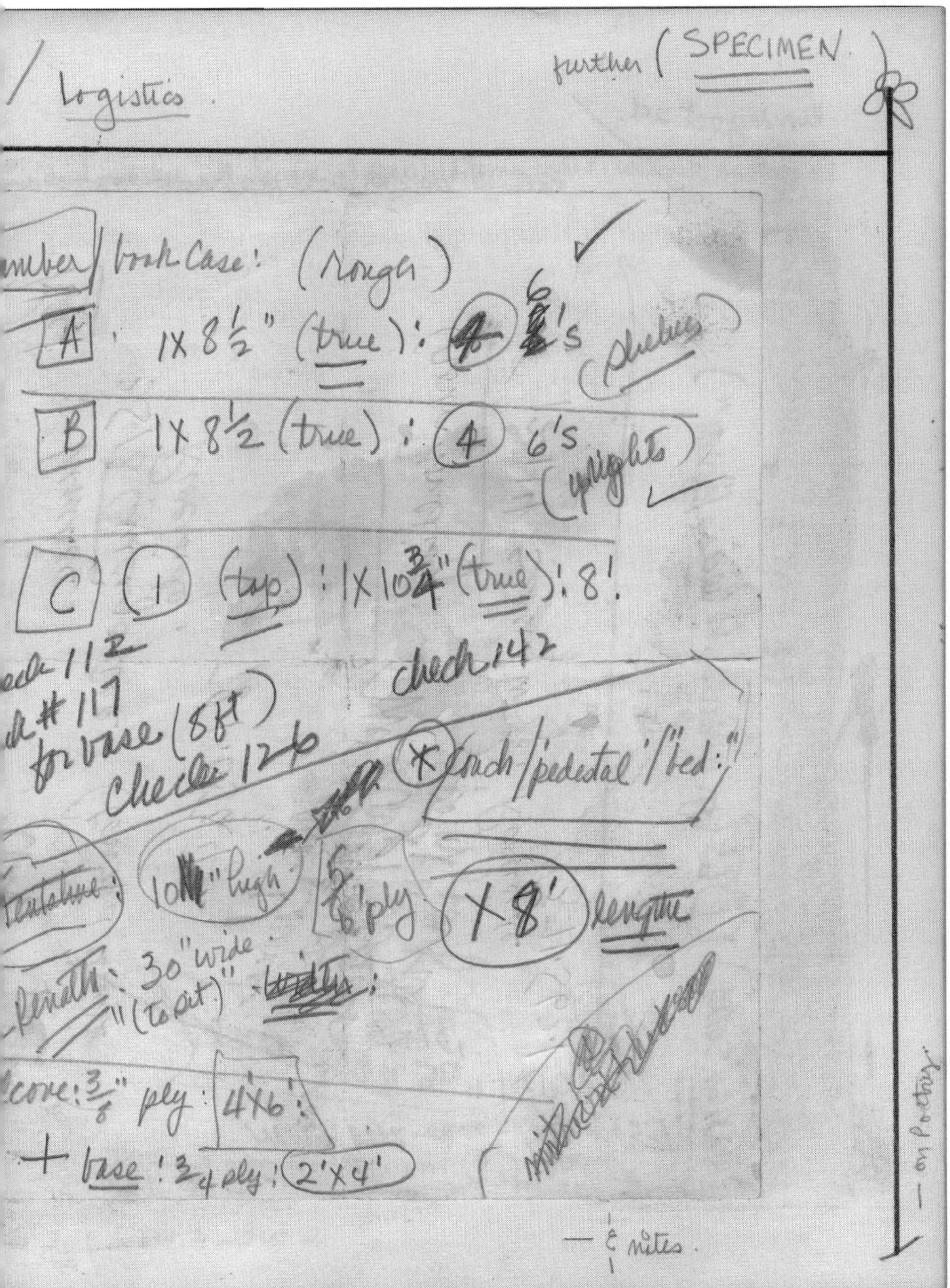

— on Poetry.

— & notes.

Untitled
October, 1988 – January, 1989
[MSS 0587   23   4]

To the Cabinet: U.B:

10 letters:

[Privy. .. <u>Platform</u> <u>Notes</u>: / for Concensus   (page one)

____

[UNCLE BOB:]

<u>Slogans</u>.

Quote.

____

POLITICS: the garrulous Adjective, everyman needs his horse.
No more Mom and apple pie; sexual proclivities are Private
1) Enterprise: God pays taxes...
No more angels; no more pins.
Punctuation is critical.
The Sentence is priority.

. . .

A pansy is pretty, a rose is a rose.
Sex is not education: deprecation is a Lie
2) made Fact. Priorities of war are good swords and
best swimmers. Language is talk.

. . .

The invention of Radio changed history;
Give television to England; Armenians made Saroyan,
World Fairs bring revenue. Teachers should speak three
3) languages. Tailors have a place. Bakers are not required
to sing opera. Letter-writing is an obligation; politics
is money.

. . .

IF is not the best equation: children sing the same songs.
4) War is sportive. Barter is a price.
Ghostwriting is requisite; profanity is counter-
Productive.

*

5) No more jogging.

*

6) A good man wears clothes, culture is spelled with a c.
Make Thanksgiving christmas... a fire under every pot, a

Untitled
February – May, 1989
[MSS 0587   24   1]

CALIFORNIA ARTS COUNCIL

1901 BROADWAY, SUITE A
SACRAMENTO, CA 95818
PHONE (916) 445-1530
FAX   (916) 327-1867

April 28, 1989

Dear Fellowship Applicant:

I am pleased to inform you that you have been recommended
for a California Arts Council Artists' Fellowship. The
panel's recommendations will be presented to the Council
in early June for their approval. You will be notified
thereafter regarding the final outcome.

Presently I am preparing a brief biographical statement
on each applicant that has been recommended for a fellowship.
It is important that you send me as soon as possible a copy
of your resume and/or a brief artistic statement. Could you
please list to date your publications: books, works that
have appeared in magazines and/or anthologies, and any awards
you have have received. Also, just a couple of sentences
regarding your work.

If you have any questions, do not hesitate to contact me.
It is very important that I receive this requested information
by May 5th.

Sincerely,

Anne Bourget
Program Administrator
Artists' Fellowship Program

III

Untitled
June – October, 1989
[MSS 0587   24   2]

* Materials (est.):

		$
2 gal enamel (oil) @ 18⁰⁰	=	36⁰⁰
9 gal flat (water) @ 14⁰⁰	=	126⁰⁰
5 gal. Thompson's water seal @ 16⁰⁰	=	80⁰⁰
4 tubes caulk	=	8⁰⁰
1 gal thinner	=	4⁰⁰
5 sheets sandpaper	=	3⁰⁰
1 gal ext spackle	=	14⁰⁰
2 rollers	=	4⁰⁰
2 (tray) liners	=	3⁰⁰
2 brushes	=	16⁰⁰
2 sm pails	=	5⁰⁰
3 (spray) sub shellac	=	15⁰⁰
1 bag rags	=	10⁰⁰

Total $324 —
+ 06% Tax: 19.50

Total: $343.50

+ another 5$ (1 qt stain, if we need it) = 5 —

Total, Materials: = $348⁰⁰

[Suggest ext color be white, as is —
with enamel trim (same color):
Custom colors wd cost more.]

— Rob Crosson.

Friday eve
October 12th, 1951

Dear Bob,

Thanks for letting me see these pieces (figure youve
read a copy of ORIGIN by now) and coming, at least, in
the direction of my needs.

They dont come off for me, any of them. Seem to work
too hard for colloquial effects and are unconvincing for
the most part. The letters have moments of quality (mis-
spellings dont ring true to me as they do in PATERSON), tho
why you call them prose and then type them as though they
were verse, I dont quite understand.

Substance isnt penetrated enough anywhere--and again the
STANZAS are best in this respect. Your rhythms are too
flat and part of yr failure is importantly in this lack
of rhythmic carry, thrust, so that a kind of boredom creeps
in.

If you keep at these things, such things, and think you
grow out of them, improving, please let me see more.

        Best Luck...

                Sincerely
                yours
                Cid Corman

Origin
a quarterly for the creation
ED. CID CORMAN, 51 JONES AVENUE
DORCHESTER 24, MASSACHUSETTS

Sunday Jan 28/90

Peter:

Just now chanced to read (latest)copies
of <u>Calliope</u>. The printer grossly fucked up.
PPg 5 and 6 are repeated, pp 9and 10 are
missing, pp. 25 & 26 are repeated, p 45
is repeated.

I'll keep what copies I have--sold two a
friend (without rereading); plus the
copies delivered to BB: one of which Laurel
Ann bought(and I signed).

Suggest they be retrieved, and deball
the fucker.

X

Bob.

Closson

———————————————————— *- copy -*

Untitled
February–April, 1990
[MSS 0587   25   1]

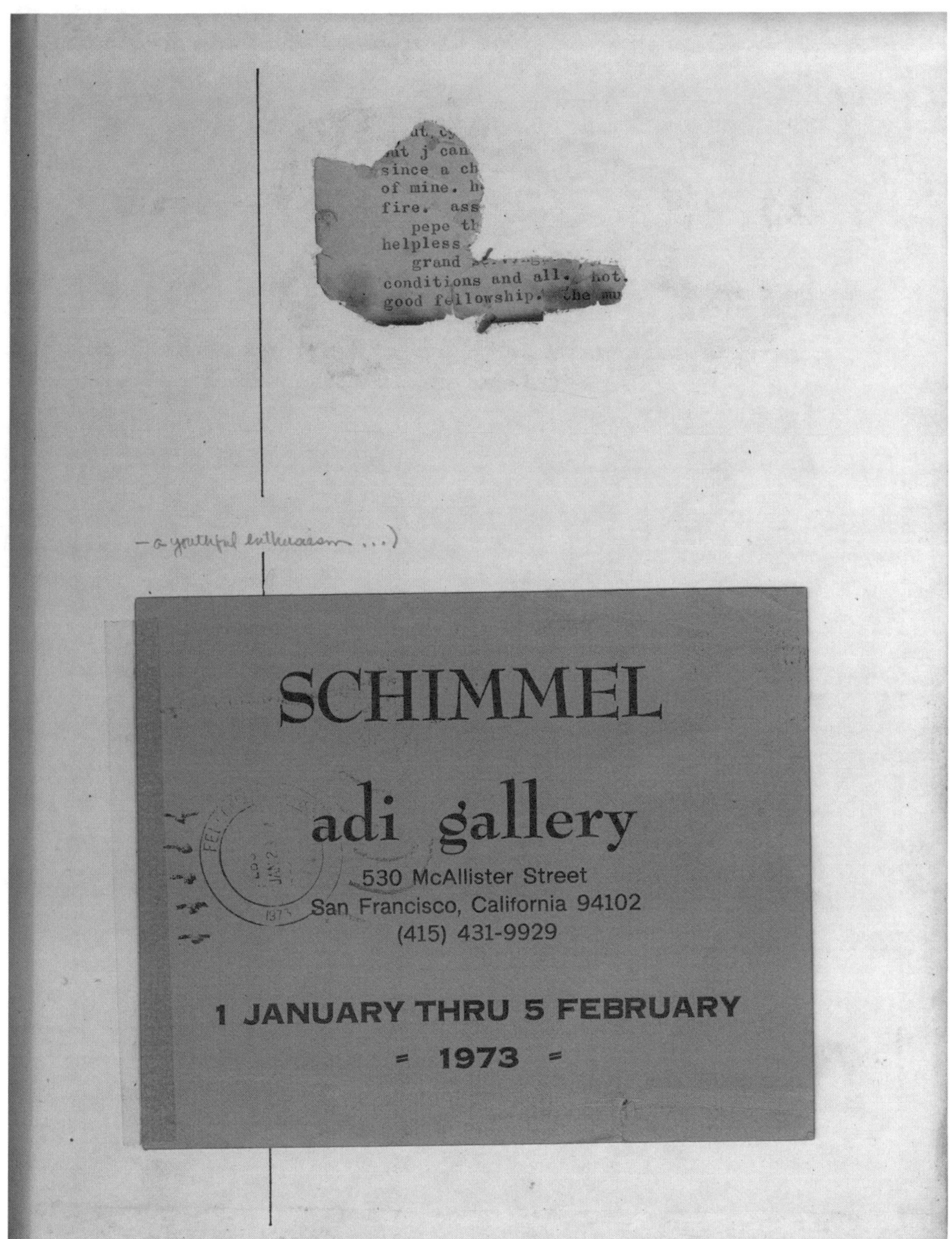
at, c
t j can
since a ch
of mine. h
fire. ass
pepe th
helpless
grand
conditions and all. hot.
good fellowship. the mu

— a youthful enthusiasm ...)

SCHIMMEL

adi gallery

530 McAllister Street
San Francisco, California 94102
(415) 431-9929

1 JANUARY THRU 5 FEBRUARY
= 1973 =

Untitled
April – June, 1990
[MSS 0587   25   2]

Monday June 4/90

Mr. Harold [Howard] Junker, ED:
ZYZZYVA—41 Sutter St.
San Francisco 94104

Mr. Junker:

Today received Mms (mine) submitted to you
by my friend Leland Hickman. I appreciate
your response.

I don't know ZYZZYVA: best see copy of it
to know what you, and it, are about.

————————

Your generous invitation—'if you felt inclined
to be so guided in giving me another chance when
the muse visits again'—is well taken. The muse
and I are inseperable. Visits, difficult; freeways,
troublesome. I like surface roads.

Thanks,

Rob
crosson

Untitled
June – July, 1990
[MSS 0587   25   3]

Dear Bob:

Enclosed, as specimen.
No return necessary.

} *today: cant xerox (work) — but will
send it on . . . when able .
— Maybe today — . . .*

____

Paul (V) came over last night; left with me the latest
<u>American</u> <u>Book</u> <u>Review</u>, and copy of your SELF PUBLISHING,
Thanks.

Helmes (however spelled--not <u>bread</u>) rallies us.
These be not best of times...

Your summary is well taken.
Small presses does seem the only way out.

____

Do, and is.
My own view is that all of us—however persevering—
have written in such a way (to cover our ass): to make
of our lives and work, something special: in my case,
'fuck audience'— (My c sticks)... Of course not at all
'fuck audience'—but, more, getting grips with whatever
talent we might have to do what we need to do, without
all the fuss (engineering) of getting it printed.

A limitation of mine.
Perhaps (some) pretentious.

____

                  yet
Daybook still lingers at Red Hill. (By this time—some
years later, it is yet to come into print.)... what I was (am)
doing in Daybook, is exactly what you say: 'publishing' my own
book, in pencil... which is not to say it's hot-stuff, but
what I daily do to make 'sense' of what's otherwise 'making
a living': which is what we all do anyway—. I guess that's
maybe (all) any poet can do.?

I'm not making much sense.
Here.   *(fuck Wallace Stevens ...)*
                                      — give him a eat .

Today phoned Holly—thanks for her book.
Told her—knowing her work--how much I admire
(envy) her 'centerdness,' a quality I seem to lack.
Holly, graciously, laughed.

Hello.

            My best to you both — Bob —

Untitled
August 2–29, 1990
[MSS 0587   26   1]

Sun & Moon Press

6148 Wilshire Boulevard
Gertrude Stein Plaza
Los Angeles, California 90048

TEL: (213) 857-1115
FAX: (213) 857-0143

August 9, 1990

Robert L. Crosson
8021 Jovenita Canyon Rd.
Los Angeles, CA 90046

Dear Robert Crosson:

Douglas wanted to write to you himself, but things are very busy at the Press, and he did not want you to wait for this letter.

Thank you very much for sending us *The Man in The Moon*. Douglas has read it and he admires the work very much.

Unfortunately, as Douglas has mentioned to you, we are completely overbooked in poetry. We are not able to take on new manuscripts at this time. Douglas wishes you the best of luck placing it elsewhere.

Sincerely,

Noah de Lissovoy
Editorial Assistant

erli, Publisher
son, Managing Editor
or, Promotion
Manager Distribution

Untitled
August – November, 1990
[MSS 0587   26   2]

149

————————————————• October 12 · Friday ————————
up. 7 am̶ rewrite ~~Bus~~ 'Riding the Bus'...
8 am: phone Jon (& Lucia): will be late, needs go
to bank... [re. 'forgery': to my account...]
9 am. Ba visits (in bathrobe) with check from John
————————————————★ (plumber's bill): (308$)...

9 ³⁰: to Bank: 'Marine' is
not in: she is due 10³⁰ am:
(re 'forgery')... to work
(at Joe's): 11 – 4³⁰ pm.

Home (traffic) 5¹⁵.

6 pm. phone Paul:
won't show: ~~am~~ tired,
irritable, and no fit
company...
(P: 'I knew you'd crap out.')
will call later...

★ Edward phones (message):
"Mum is back in the
hospital. We don't expect
her to last the night."
will call...
[6³⁰ pm.] Have plugged phone in.

6⁴⁵: phone Edward ('Butch'):
(cellular phone): no answer.

CAMP DAVID

A Oct 90

Dear Bobbett—
        This seems high for
replacing a washer — but
if you figure it will work
for a while — okay.
        Hope all's well. Talked
to Otis the other day and he
sent his love to you.
        Say hello to the gang —
            ever — Loops

(—— specimen.)

Untitled
November, 1990 – February, 1991
[MSS 0587   26   3]

and can cough, only bending over.

———————————————

10:15 am. Dr. Bob phones:
. can I visit tomorrow?
(vasomolds).

yes.

11:30 am. phone Pierre (Pasinetti): hello~
did he get my fliers? (poetry readings).
He did not... tells me
Franchesca has gone back to teach at Georgetown
University; was "desolate" we couldn't
get together while she was here...

We will be in touch.

*

Bills, off.

*

12:50 am. Dick Simon phones: wants me
(when available) to repaint his kitchen
cabinets...

Untitled
February – June, 1991
[MSS 0587   26   4]

First Class: by way of hello.

Buy paints, et al, for Ghetto Flats.
(Some guilty I've not been there —: ($) —
toss priorities . . .

(Bills, for the moment, paid.) . . .
— Commence, a/m . . . : "Ghetto Flats", in hand.
Christine : /
"Versus birds—in—the bush :
                        nag nag."

(maybe).

*

⁊⅂⌐: hear swell music: solo/lad,
singing (in Spanish) :— at the same
time whistles . . . . at first thought —
it a neighbor's record . . . lovely.

It's one of Rudy's (young) workers:
hatchelering (sp > the dead trees . . .
(Just up the path, beyond the (blooming)
geraniums . . .)

a young lad.
(I just snuck a look at him .)
Some skinney for the job.

*   5³⁰ phone Dianne (Ayimov) Senior :
(213·654·3075) to give number of
Carpenters : Urman & Marthel (Dr. B's friends) :
(Bob Marthel) : # work : 818·508·0534 · (7³⁰ – 5³⁰ pm.)
for her closets . . . (Have spoken, hellos, to Bob.) M.

Untitled
June – September, 1991
[MSS 0587   27   1]

INTERINSURANCE EXCHANGE of the

Automobile Club of Southern California

PROCESSING CENTER: P.O. BOX 25001 ▪ SANTA ANA, CALIFORNIA 92799-5001

June 3, 1991

T. S. Eliot
8021 Jovenita Cyn.
Los Angeles, CA 90046

RE: Return Check File Number: 89-324125
       Balance Due: $58.00   Dept. 13

Dear Mr. Eliot:

I am writing in regard to your check dated May 7, 1991, which was
written for membership fees. The check was returned by the bank
marked "Payment Stopped".

If there is any reason for the stop payment on this check that
Collections has not been made aware of, please contact me at the
number shown below. However, if you no longer wish to retain
your membership, simply return your card in order to clear your
account.

Enclosed is a courtesy envelope for your mailing convenience.

Jean Gmeiner
Collections, P136
Telephone: (714) 850-5077
Hours: 9:00 a.m. - 5:00 p.m.
Monday-Friday

JG:jr

Enclosure

Untitled
September – December, 1991
[MSS 0587   27   2]

CONS

College of Neglected Science

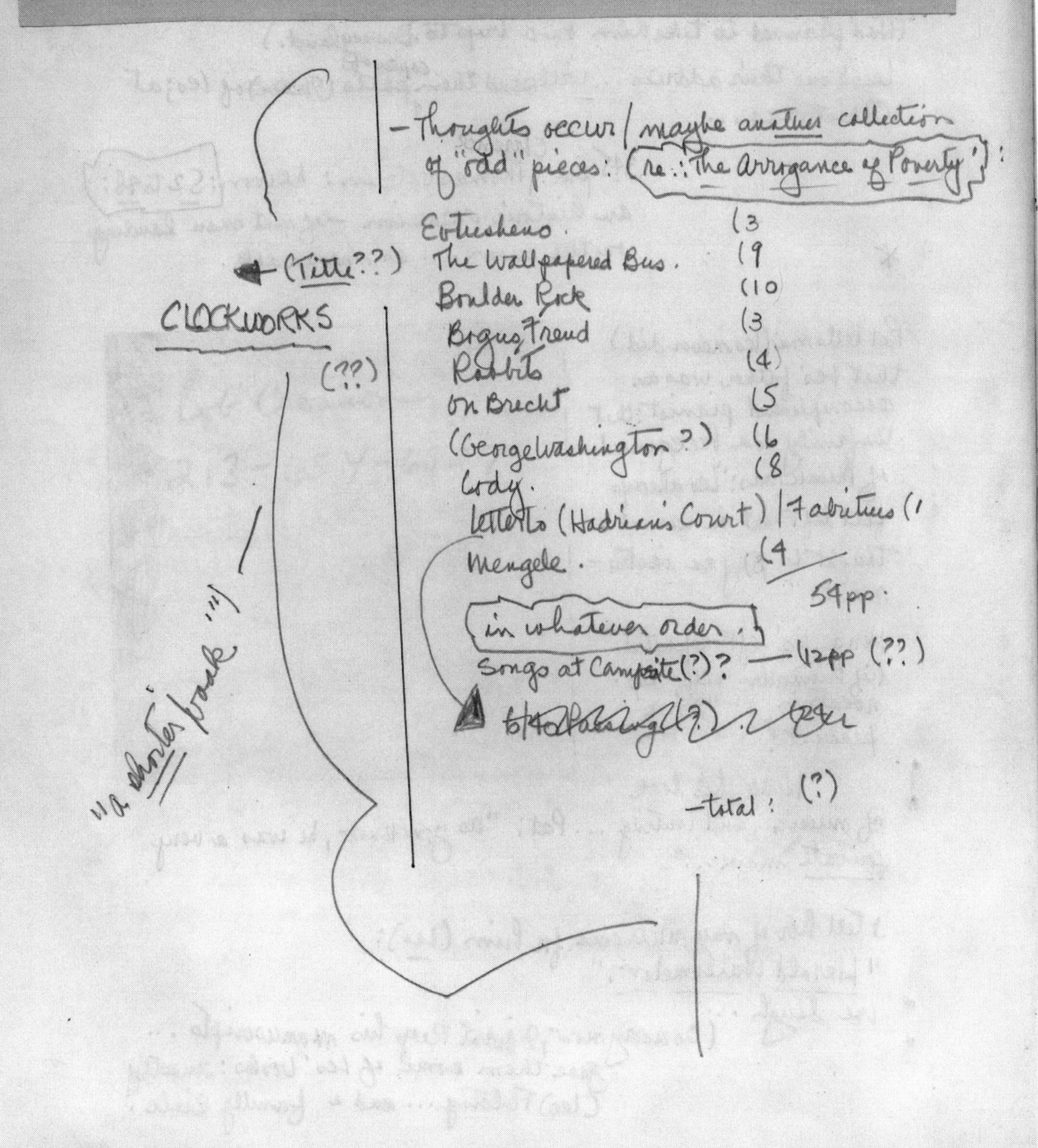

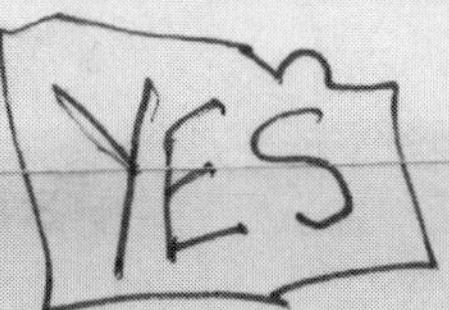

Rough: 12.15.9

Pier Paolo Pasolini—_Uccellacci_ & _Uccellini_
(_Sparrows_ & Hawks), 1964

His last black-and-white film, I'm told.
I liked it.
  —Carl Dreiser

A wretched, mawkish piece.
  —Howard Hawks

Krieg ist Feuchtbar.
  —Robert Wiene

  Few films have 'changed my life'; prime, among them,
Bergman's _Persona_—his film took me 'out of my life',
shocked me to realization that I—I suppose it could be said,
A Provincial American (perhaps redundant)—had more to learn
about the world than what was (and is) purported in most
Hollywood (hence, Domestic) films. Fellini, likewise.
Pasolini, in particular.

  I don't read Italian, I am dependant upon sub-titles...
Fellini mesmerized me—I needn't speak the language: what
images purported on the screen spoke for themselves—in my
sense (maybe thanks to Resnais), ala comic-strips... boxes
of faces, changing. Fellini did that in large chunks—
Pasolini, not.

  I grew up on the films of Frank Capra—ultimate sanctuary
of The American Dream... no 'changing-boxes' (visually speaking):
few unexpected surprises... The Medium of the Film left to
strictly Narrative story-telling. Noticeably linear. Bergman
did away with that. Pasolini, in _Sparrows & Hawks_, turns the
tables on us. His framing is linear—much like Chaucer's
Canterbury Tales—but at the same time, abruptly comic-strip.

Untitled
March – May, 1992
[MSS 0587   27   4]

For every opportune reason —

    Dr. Bob typewrites a letter:
(envelope)
      to U.C.L.A.

    Yeah.

      And yes.
      And yes.

    Say hellos —

Dr. B. (yet) speaks in a
whisper … I find me whispering
backs —:
me: "Does this (my whispering)
offend you?"
Dr. B: "It isn't necessary."

(Dr. B. shows me — 'paint-repair'-
work he wants done on backside, exterior,
house: what (to me) looks like
an 'object-thrown': — with some
force…)

    — from the looks of it, less
a hard object, then something plant,
or vegetable.

Untitled
May–July, 1992
[MSS 0587   28   1]

21.

*

7pm. phone (message): Rudy Rodriguez (brush-
clearance), re estimate of worke here (on Jovenita)
to be done - vis-a-vie - Fire-Inspection notice . . .
Hetloes. (Brush-clearance, et al . . .) and dead trees.

*

ROBERT CROSSON

Painting

8021 JOVENITA L.A. 90046
213-654-6527

— to Dion.

CONS

College of Neglected Science

August 1, 1992

TO: Governor William Clinton
    Candidate of the Democratic Party for the Presidency
        of the United States

WHEREAS your political will seems considerable and matched only by
   the triteness and banality of your political thought;

VISION is a tight mouth of smiling teeth and a motorcycle passing;
   God is baseball;

WHEREAS your pretensions to economic democracy, social justice and,
   above all, freedom of speech appear to be boundless;

COURAGE is money in the bank; tailors make clothes;

WHEREAS you have swung the Democratic Party once more to the right
   while being at heart a liberal who, like other liberals, is laden
   with conscience and rather light on courage;

THERE is every good reason to change the format of the dollar but
   the Treasury says no; that Eye they got;

WHEREAS your candicacy, two weeks after the Party convention, has
   the potential to be successful and, once in office, you do seem
   capable of even more vigorous destruction to our political and
   economic system than the incumbent candidate;

ABOVE the Pyramid; and the American assumption that the Wild West
   has made us Heroes;

WHEREAS your 'covenant' with the American people promises, in its
   historically unfortunate choice of terms, an enthusiastic, pious
   and pale future for this country;

IN the old days we had cream in pitchers and sugar in a jar;

we hereby endorse your candidacy for President of the United States
   in 1992.

('etcetera' being good word to define ...)

A

Margaret whiting.

like fishes, performing / the aquarium

Aint she sweet — / see her walking down the street

apple & aunts —
(etcetera) —
Heartaches, and people singing songs (by
others) made famous
trips to the moon
(under a false bottom) —
sea - life.

Yes indeed.
yes. a flattery of applause.
Even with small audience,
good to hear the clap.
~~xxxxxxxxxxx~~ not of one
Hand. When things, afoot become
a threaded screw.... a place
to hunt

Now I ask you
(very confidentially)

*

Not to make much sense of it.
or fit

Fish & aquarium.

aint.

She.

*

Shep (Ralph's) 10:25 pm
Deck, 11.
(no call from John.)
— phone Richard, to say so.

*

Untitled
October – December, 1992
[MSS 0587   28   4]

, Desert Storm ,
(of. deep ^with men on the moon / and latest exhibit of
' Treasures of the ottoman Empire .'
In Westwood. —

ROBERT L. CROS..N
3132 BERKELEY CIRCLE
LOS ANGELES, CA 90026

ROBERT L. CROSSON
3132 BERKELEY CIRCLE
LOS ANGELES, CA 90026

CROSSON
3132 BERKELEY CIRCLE
LOS ANGELES, CA 90026

~ new stamps ...

Sunday Nov. 8th : Work De Mari's 9-11³⁰ am:
install wallpaper: 'border' on kitchen
walls... Collect bill.

*

Shop, Vons (Sunset - Virgil) ...
Home, 2 pm.

* Paul visits ; pays bills. we share
drinks ...

5 pm: to El Coyote: meet mary alice ('Emm'),
Joe & Lauri (Dupuis). Eats... xxxxxx
Joe & lauri will emmigrate to Canada,
(Joe's birthplace) next March: officials
have held up paper-work... Emm has
a new hair-do. lauri has lost weight.
(wears white jacket & white overalls;
with a glittering broach...)
Home at seven... reread stuff to
read, on Wednesday... 8³⁰: to bed...

———— phone Irene Salinger
(at Ferndell Place): her "lectures"
went well: has had trouble living
help to move boxes: one has
told her he has aids... will be
in touch, as soon as house is
cleared...

— from P. 100 —

NATIONAL
ENDOWMENT
FOR THE
ARTS

*The Federal agency
that supports the
visual, literary and
performing arts to
benefit all Americans*

Arts in Education

Challenge &
Advancement

Dance

Design Arts

Expansion Arts

Folk Arts

International

Literature

Locals

Media Arts

Museum

Music

Opera/Musical
Theater

Presenting &
Commissioning

State & Regional

Theater

Visual Arts

The Nancy Hanks Center
1100 Pennsylvania Ave. NW
Washington, DC 20506
202/682-5400

February 8, 1993

Mr. Robert Crosson
8021 Jovenita Canyon Rd.
Los Angeles, CA 90046

Dear Mr. Crosson,

Thank you for your telephone call on February 1, 1993 requesting comments on your application A-92-009134.

The panel which reviewed your manuscript felt that the series of prose poems was loose, wandering, and resembled a monologue. Panelists commented that the use of the prose poem seemed an excuse for a lack of form rather than developing structure within the form. The panel characterized the writing as undistinguished and self-indulgent. In poems such as "City of Angeles," the absence of any clues to the identity of the speaker prevented the reader from becoming fully engaged. Finally, the panel felt that your manuscript did not distinguish itself from the many other submissions under consideration.

For the 1993 fellowships, the Literature Program received 2,370 eligible applications and awarded 89 grants, a funding rate of 3.6 percent. Due to the limited amount of funds available, many applications of merit were turned down. Please remember that each year the composition of the panel changes, and another panel may have a different response to your work.

I hope this information will prove useful. Thank you for your interest in the National Endowment for the Arts.

Sincerely,

Alexander Ooms
Creative Writing Fellowships
Literature Program

Untitled
April – June, 1993
[MSS 0587   29   2]

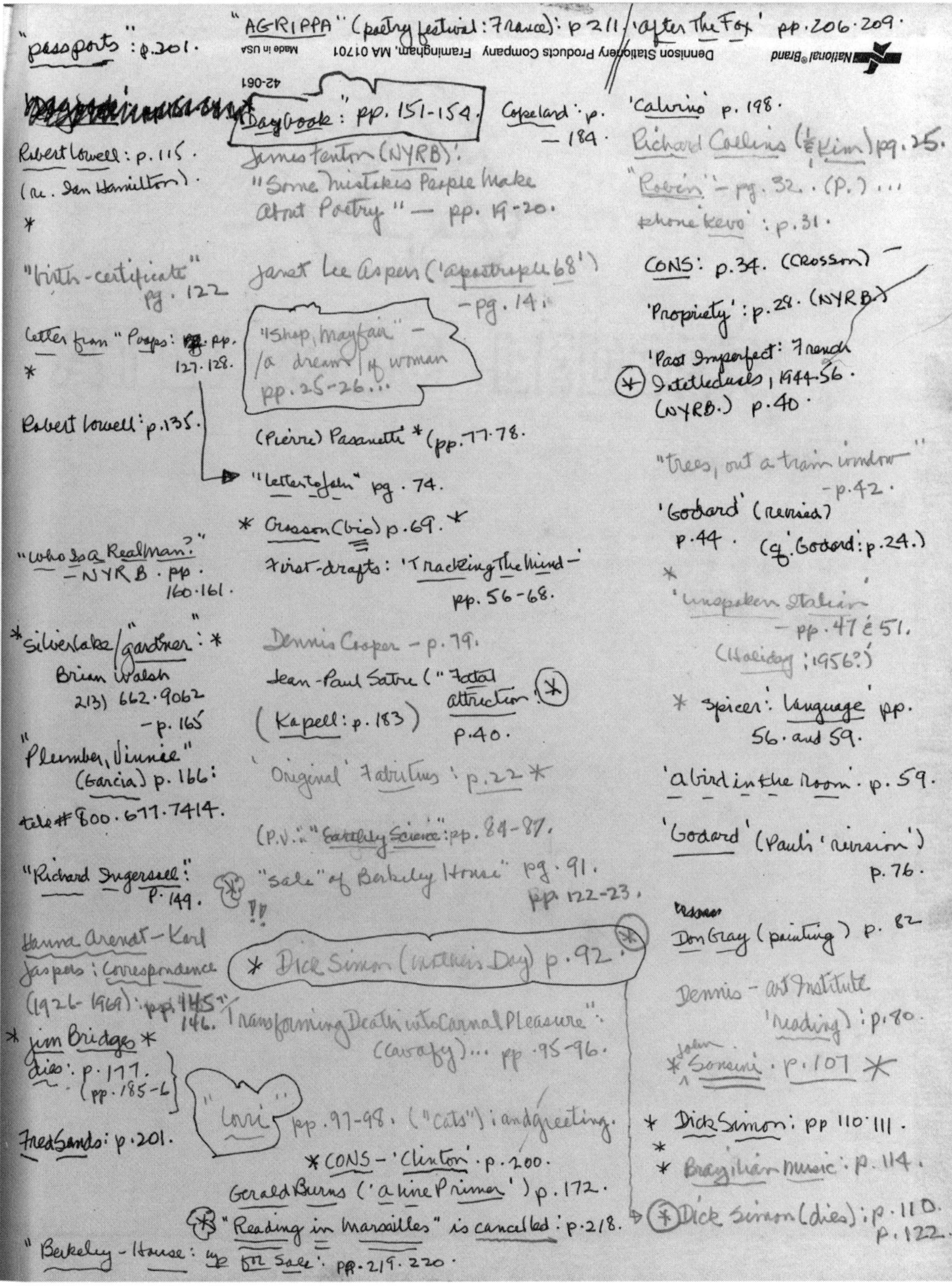

"passports": p.201.

"AGRIPPA" (poetry festival: France): p.211 / 'after The Fox', pp.206-209.

"Daybook": pp. 151-154.   Copeland: p. -184

'Calvino' p.198.

Robert Lowell: p.115.
(re. Ian Hamilton).
*

James Fenton (NYRB):
"Some Mistakes People Make
About Poetry" — pp.19-20.

Richard Collins (½ Kim) pg.25.

"Robin" - pg.32. (P.) ...

phone Kevo: p.31.

"birth-certificate" pg.122

Janet Lee Aspens ('apostrophe 68') — pg.14.

CONS: p.34. (Crosson) —

'Propriety': p.28. (NYRB)

Letter from "Poops": pp. 127-128.
*

"Shop, Mayfair" —
/a dream/ of woman
pp.25-26...

'Past Imperfect: French
Intellectuals, 1944-56.
(NYRB.) p.40.

Robert Lowell: p.135.

(Pierre) Pasanetti * (pp.77-78.

"letter to John" pg.74.

"trees, out a train window"
- p.42.
'Godard' (revised)
p.44.   (cf. 'Godard: p.24.)
*

"who Is a Real Man?"
— NYRB. pp. 160-161.

* Crosson (bio) p.69. *
First-drafts: 'Tracking The Mind' —
pp.56-68.

'unspoken Italian'
- pp. 47 & 51.
(Holiday: 1956?)

* Silverlake/gardner: *
Brian Walsh
213) 662-9062
- p.165

Dennis Cooper — p.79.

Jean-Paul Satre ("Fatal
attraction")
(Kapell: p.183)   p.40.

* Spicer: language pp.
56. and 59.

"Plumber, Vinnie"
(Garcia) p.166:
tele# 800-677-7414.

'Original' Fabritus: p.22 *

'a bird in the room'. p.59.

(P.V.: "Earthly Science": pp.84-87.

'Godard' (Paul's 'version')
p.76.

"Richard Ingersoll":
p.149.

"sale" of Berkeley House: pg.91.
pp 122-23.

Don Gray (painting) p.82

Hanna Arendt—Karl
Jaspers: Correspondence
(1926-1969): pp.145-146.

* Dick Simon (Mother's Day) p.92.

"Transforming Death into Carnal Pleasure":
(Cavafy)... pp.95-96.

Dennis - art Institute
'reading': p.80.

* jim Bridges *
dies: p.177.
[pp.185-6]

* Sorrini: p.107 *

Fred Sands: p.201.

"Lori": pp.97-98. ("Cats") i and greeting.

* CONS - 'Clinton'. p.200.

Gerald Burns ('a nine Primer') p.172.

* Dick Simon: pp 110-111.
*

* Brazilian music. p.114.

"Reading in Marseilles" is cancelled: p.218.

* Dick Simon (dies): p.110.
p.122.

"Berkeley-House: up for Sale". pp.219-220.

Untitled
June – August, 1993
[MSS 0587   29   3]

LAST QUARTETS

> From each according to his ability,
> to each according to his need.

>   (Pronoun in question)

Tigers do not burn bright.
Slim Pickens is a real name.

The question is not Are Poets Whores?—
but what Horse rode them to the Capitol?
(accessory to the Formal parade—

Being more accustomed to the race track.)

The Piano is a percussive instrument.
Of.
Ambitious Bureaucrats
who have lost count of their Drawers
Or decorative Doilies

(Tenor and Tone at case).
And/or the Poet
who might never have had one.

A picture of Mussolini playing the violin.
Listening to Caruso on the Victorola.

'Sins of My Old Age' was written by Rossini—
bourne of a disperate Clime; and Diet.
Leafy Salads (one feels) Beethoven
never ate.

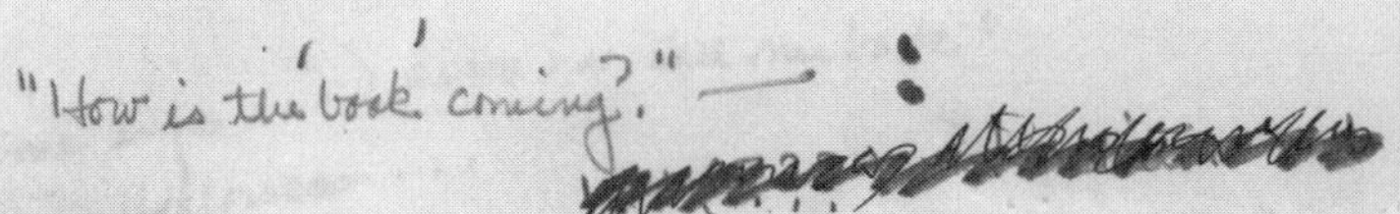

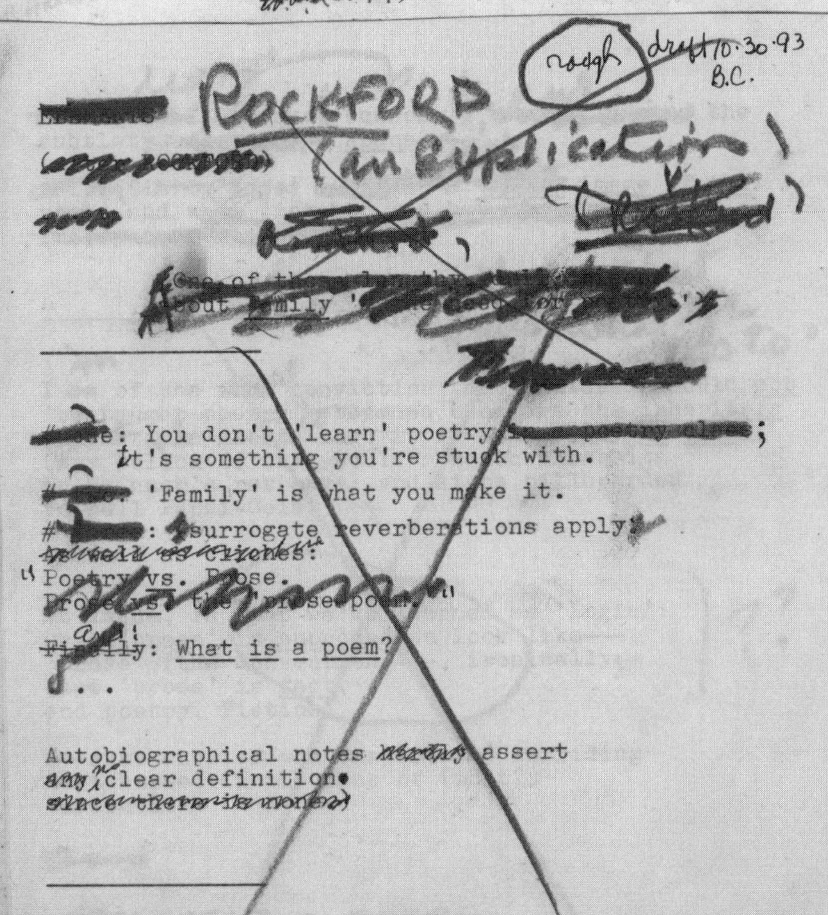

#One: You don't 'learn' poetry in poetry class;
   it's something you're stuck with.

#Two: 'Family' is what you make it.

#Three: surrogate reverberations apply.

"Poetry vs. Prose.
Prose vs. the 'prose poem.'"

Finally: What is a poem?

. . .

Autobiographical notes assert
any clear definition.

First of all (should it be your proclivity) you
read a lot. (When I say 'read', I mean you're
looking for something, though you might not know
what you're looking for.) After years of reading,
you begin to understand what a sentence is, and
the importance of punctuation.
After a while you learn to spell.

All along, you copy quotes
from books you like & post them on the wall
above the typewriter (in my day, it was a type-
writer) as inspiration.

After assembling a (long) catalogue of 'inspiration',
you go on with the same work you've been doing

Untitled
November – December, 1993
[MSS 0587   30   3]

following pages: *Untitled*
December, 1993 – February, 1994
[MSS 0587   31   1]

RES SACRUM

A roof is a roof you can count on.
A woman is more beautiful.

Those monks (who sheared the sheep)
bathed & legs, to stomp the grapes,
and are carried) ...
peering down rock holes
to light a candle.

Later, to sacrifice a ram
(decked in flowers)
the elder women cooked.

*

while workmen dyed the wool
in bats (they stirred with rakes)
and plopped to stone premise.
For the women to gather
and weave tapestries.

To be washed, and walked upon!
in pointed shoes, or bare feet.
or worn as collars.

referents ...?

11.25.93.

— with cookies:
— from Maria ...

(12·23·93.

The RI
scheduled fo
12/9/93, has
due to a lack

event
his evening,
en cancelled
illumination.

THE COLLEGE.

BERKELEY · DAVIS · IRVINE · LOS ANGELES · RIVERSIDE · SAN DIEGO · SAN FRANCISCO

SANTA BARBARA · SANTA CRUZ

DEPARTMENT OF ITALIAN
405 HILGARD AVENUE
LOS ANGELES, CALIFORNIA 90024-1535
FAX: (310) 206-7727
(310) 825-1940

25 April 1994

Mr. Robert Crosson
3132 Berkeley Circle
Los Angeles, CA 90026

Dear Mr. Crosson:

On behalf of the Department of Italian, it is my pleasure to invite you to participate in "The Disappearing Pheasant 2", the second in a series of symposia on contemporary American and Italian poetry, which will take place November 3 - 6, 1994, here at UCLA. The three-day event will feature some thirty poets from the U.S. and Italy in a series of panels and readings.

A partial list of sponsors for the symposium includes the Ahmanson Foundation, the Italian Cultural Institute, the Getty Center for the History of Art and the Humanities, the UCLA Critical Studies and Human Sciences Program, Sun and Moon Press, and Ribot. This event follows the successful appearance of the first "Disappearing Pheasant" held at New York University in October 1992.

Among the poets invited to this latest manifestation are: John Ashbery, Nanni Balestrini, Amiri Baraka, Biagio Cepollaro, Michelle Clinton, Norma Cole, Robert Crosson, Milo De Angelis, Biancamaria Frabotta, Alfredo Giuliani, Milli Graffi, Barbara Guest, Lynn Hejinian, Angelo Lumelli, Mario Luzi, Giancarlo Majorino, Douglas Messerli, Giulia Niccolai, Rosanna Ombres, Elio Pagliarani, Michael Palmer, Dennis Phillips, Martha Ronk, Jerome Rothenberg, Giovanna Sandri, Edoardo Sanguineti, Leslie Scalapino, Gilbert Sorrentino, Nathaniel Tarn and Paul Vangelisti. There will also be a handful of critics invited from each country.

We will be able to offer you round-trip transportation between your home and Los Angeles, five days accommodations in the Westwood area of Los Angeles, meals, and a modest honorarium of $200. We wish the latter might be more, but budgetary constraints, and above all, our desire to enlarge the symposium, make a larger sum infeasible.

If you are able to attend, please complete the attached confirmation form and return it to our offices via fax or mail as soon as possible. We would appreciate an answer to our invitation no later than May 15, as publicity and logistical exigencies are hard upon us. If you are a foreign national, we will forward any necessary visa documents in order that you might enter the country with a working visa, and flight arrangements will be made at a later date.

Untitled
May – June, 1994
[MSS 0587   31   3]

hereinto: (??):

CONS

College of Neglected Science
May 18,94

OF EMPIRE

Whitey go down the road be okay with me.
I be here anyway him gone or not: him
on his high horse: be time he go...
I borne white aint my fault.
Voices I can't fix
say good riddance.

I be tired of him: his dumb talk...
Thinks he owns the sidewalk.
I be working man.
I be what them schoolboys write about.
Whitey go down the road okay with me.

I got a house: I got a inside toilet...
can't read don't make me less:
put my eyes to it I can name half the weeds
this side any big highway.
I got kids.

I do good at the plant.
I work regular.

PREAMBULUM

<u>I'm a sonofabitch</u>: the weight of import shifts in
context...<u>i.e.</u>: that Maxim suggests its opposite,
given another person or place in time...an inter-
esting if curious phenomenon: that what we hold
Right and True is, for some (perhaps fickle, perhaps
not), solely and predictably dependent upon our
instruction of invariably propitious Example...
that is: what's good for the goose is not necessarily
good for: a suggestion of further clichés. That it's
alright to be rich if you're famous (for what is up-
held right reason) and that a king or queen has right
to be capricious because they are in another League
or Drawingroom.

Untitled
July – September, 1994
[MSS 0587   32   1]

Lorem ipsum dolor sit amet, consectetur adipscing elit, sed diam nonumy eiusmod
tempor incidunt ut laboree et dolore magna aliquam erat valupat. Ut eiusmad ad
minimim veniami quis nostrd exercitaion ullamcorpor suscipit laboris nisi ut aliquip
ex ea commodo consequat.
SPQR: sono porci questi romani OR such pigs, these romans.

9 July 1994

Dear Bob,

The old & the new on one page. The First Type out of
my printer. Nonsense lines courtesy of Dale Gullicksen
to which I added the initials on the Roman battle banners:
SPQR (senatus populusque romani) rendered as such pigs...
	Enclosing the draft page in tribute to our departed. I
sent one to Dennis Dybeck and got in yesterday's post these (7/6/94)
3 pages. I thought you'd be touched by them.
	So here I am typing off a brief message to you, hoping
all is well. The work begins.

John

July 18th ——————————— Monday —

Sat { (16) house-showing — Le Rustic ...
           * (write) (going nuts...)
Sun { (17) visit Martha (1³⁰) for keys
       (to Escarpa) * write ... (further, nuty) ...
       — home, watch Dodger Stadium (repeat)
       of Pavorati at Dodgers — (in every sense,
       a 'large theater'; I like it a lot.

*   (18) 10ᵖᵐ / home from Mayfair: phone
** call (message) from Paul: "just
   checking in" ...
       — finish piece!♭!
   (*) (of new pie: "Ensemble:
                        3 pp...)
(earlier, phone Martha: ~~karewetts~~
   (— departs for Italy LAX tonight at 9 pm.)
   — mail response (SAG receipts / 93 residuals!
   to (Mr.) Frazier (free postage!) ...

Untitled
October – November, 1994
[MSS 0587   32   2]

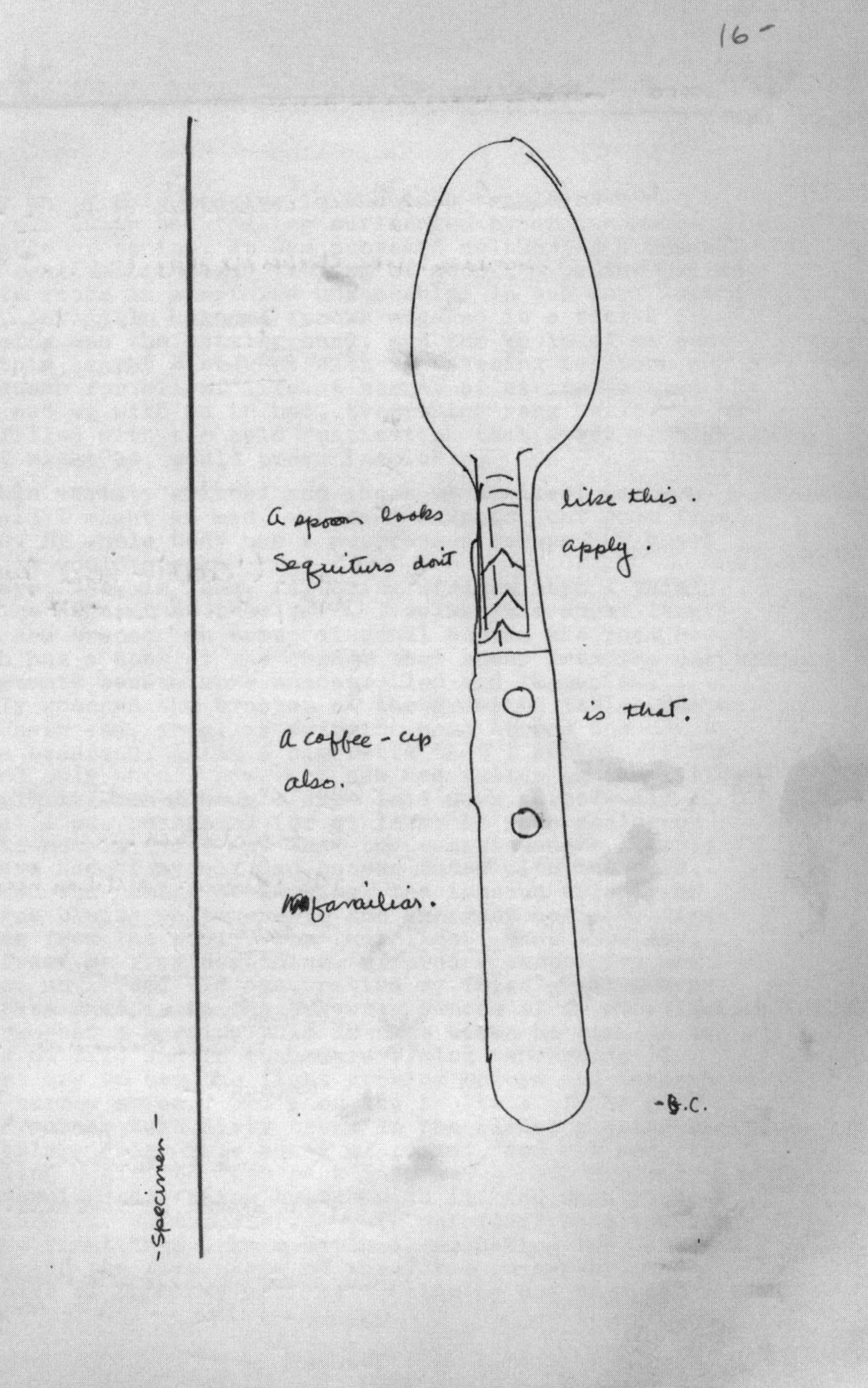
A spoon looks   like this.
Sequiturs don't   apply.

A coffee - cup   is that.
also.

familiar.

- B.C.

- Specimen -

Untitled
November, 1994 – January, 1995
[MSS 0587   32   3]

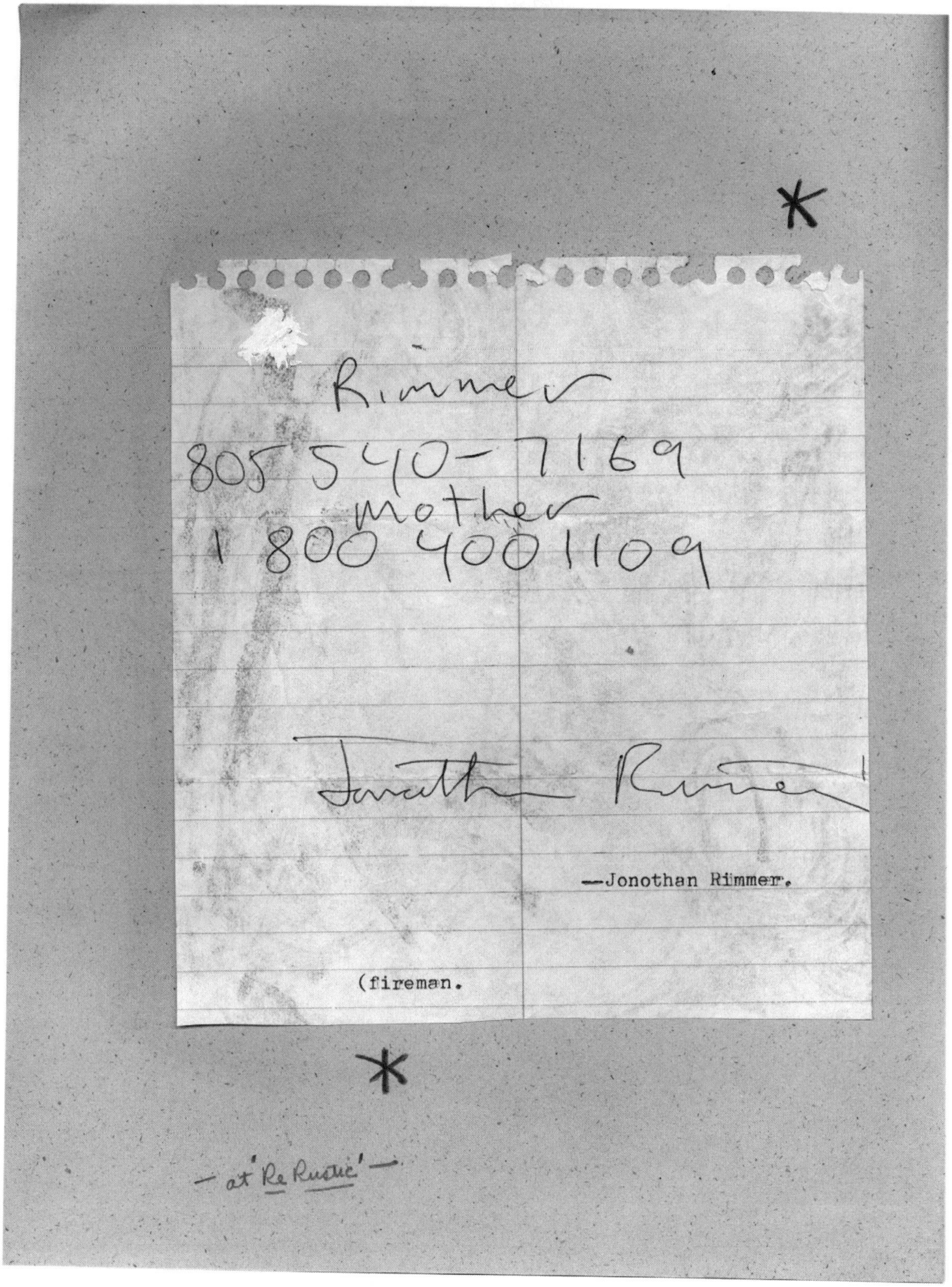

*

Rimmer
805 540-7169
mother
1 800 4001109

Jonathan Rimmer

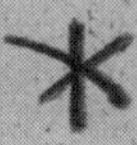

—Jonothan Rimmer.

(fireman.

*

—at 'Re Rustic'—

Untitled
January–April, 1995
[MSS 0587   33   1]

- To Douglas -   [Title ??]   [Diane : S+M.]

crosson

1. THE DAY SAM GOLDWYN STEPPED OFF THE TRAIN   (6)

2. LEMON   (1)

3. RABBITS   (2)

4. CODY   12)

5. EGYPT   6)

6. VIEW OF TOLEDO   3)

7. YEVTUSHENKO IS A FAKE HE SAYS   3)

8. CATACROCK   3)

9. BOGUS DIARIES OF S. FREUD   4)

10. SPENDING ALL NIGHT IN THE TUNNEL   1)

11. GOING UP HILL TO FETCH A PAIL OF   1)

12. I CHING   1)

13. THE IDES OF MARCH   1)

14. THE CHIEF USE OF MEN OVER FORTY-FIVE   1)

15. THE ADVANTAGE OF FORT BRAGG   4)

16. THE RED ONION   1)

17. TWO MEN IN A BOAT   2)

18. THE MAN AT THE MORTUARY   2)

19. TURKEY TROT   6)

20. MENGELE   3)

21. UPON FINDING A HAT IN THE BIRDCAGE   1)

22. ICARUS OR BARKING UP TWELVE WRONG TREES   1)

23. CAESAR   2)

24. JULY 4   1)

25. THE MAN IN THE MOON   1)

26. VILLA   2)

Untitled
May, 1995
[MSS 0587   33   2]

20$ Cash: buy gas . . . Spend afternoon at Re Rustic
(and, later — (briefly) — Drawing Room . (Henry arrives):
Pooch phones from Re Rustic to inform that a
squad-car has come by (they've busted a guy on a
motor-cycle, parked on Hillhurst, in front of my
truck (in parking-lot).) I'm pissed — : walk
back to Re Rustic to check: Paul greets me . . .
I move (repark) truck; Greet Pooch (worried about
his car [we are parked in a private parking-lot]:
Paul (with new mustache) sagely suggests the police-car
(and (single) officer is, less — out for 'bad parking' than
'potential-drunks': advises I not walk crosswalks
back to Truck; but do: obstreperous, and some paranoid:
Re-Enter Rustic (Paul departs); have 2 coffees; and drive
back (home) via Hollywood Blvd — with thanks to ' Gypsie
— Mafia ' (Harvey) who, congenially suggests that "if
I'm too drunk to crawl home", he will drive me.
His jocularity aside, he means it.
I edit the back way ——— (not at all drunk) —
but (Cautiously) realize I need go to & join John
and find I have shot my ~~precious~~ shirts (thank
god I have worn them) and exhaust list role of
toilet paper . . . in process.
Saving face.
If not premise . . .
Back to Louis', 7 pm .
no one is home .
            Lydia arrives at ~~midnite~~ 7³⁰ : takes supper;
departs at 8⁴⁵, inquiring if I've heard from her
mother.
            I
~~&c~~ have not.
            9-9³⁰ I play the (out-of-tune)
            grande piano — and feed cats .
   ⨍   (find I can still find (looking

Untitled
June, 1995 – February, 1996
[MSS 0587   33   3]

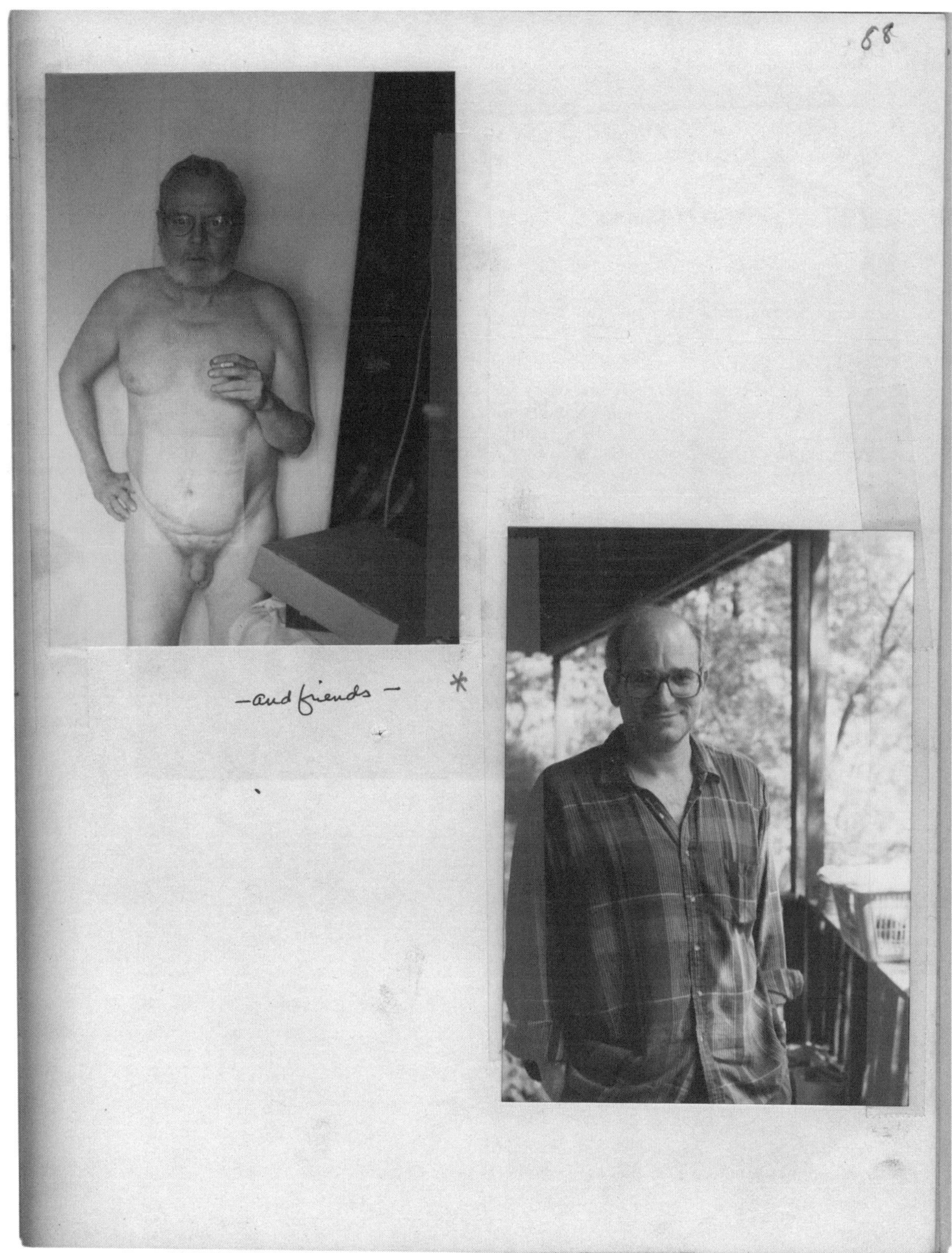

—and friends —   *

and are deliverd to Court (a long way across town).
We' ordered to exit bus (a lady cop driving).
I find it hard to navigate (I cannot navigate steps) —
  Outside — officers orders to come out fast.
  I can't. (I pull at the chains). Black gentleman
  in front of me, in face of the order, retorts: "We're
  coming — but this old man is holding us up."
  I have trouble getting off bus.
am led to another cell ... en route, handcuffs
removed. bus-driver sees my arm bleeding — calls
paramedics — they arrive (I'm put in a cubicle.) am
treated — given a larger (big) cell — solo. (It (empty) is
a ladies' cell — with boks of Kotex (I at first thought were
tapes — or books — but were not.)).
        Am taken to another cell. ('To Court').
there are 25 of us — we wait two hours.
my name is called: am, with others, 'body-searched' —
in corridor — (policewomen in plastic gloves...) me,
with a policeman who frisked me, felt my ass and
balls — rather thorough.

am subsequently called to interview by public defender (a fine lady)
told I have 3 options: plead guilty, not — or:
no contest.

I prefer the latter.

Do so.

Enter court.

  judge addresses me.
  I respond: not contest.

LOS ANGELES POLICE DEPARTMENT
VISITOR
DATE ___ JAIL FLOOR ___
LAPD 15.22.0

    Am released.   Find truck (yet) parked at curb.
** Paul picks me up...   *** (He has borrowed
  * Celebrate with a drink at Rustic.
  $500 cash — from Kevin — to bail me out — not needed)...

  * Home (Cerro Gordo) 430 pm.(?)
  Nino visits (with bottle of wine (he drinks).
  We celebrate: Helloes. He phones Martha: will

Untitled
August – October, 1996
[MSS 0587   34   2]

2: pm ~~[crossed out]~~

concoction, in context; some
~~implies a~~ ~~[crossed out]~~ frustration.
Properly in place.
* writers ~~[crossed out]~~ maybe, ~~[crossed out]~~ ~~[crossed out]~~.
~~[crossed out]~~ living alone, ~~[crossed out]~~
Especially. ~~[crossed out]~~.

(~~[crossed out]~~ ("...") address
* ~~[crossed out]~~ little way to ~~[crossed out]~~ the
                                        not.
lyric when you're ~~[crossed out]~~ ~~[crossed out]~~
hold ~~[crossed out]~~ sidelines
  ^

* * * ~~[crossed out]~~
        and
~~[crossed out]~~ swimming."
~~[crossed out]~~ pretty much land-
locked. "~~[crossed out]~~ foot to path" is ~~[crossed out]~~ some
Romantic; ~~[crossed out]~~

Talking | face to face, ~~is~~ ~~[crossed out]~~ more
comfortable. The Russians (perhaps),
~~[crossed out]~~ stolid, ~~[crossed out]~~ sincere; the French ~~[crossed out]~~ with
a sense of "humor"; the Germans
~~[crossed out]~~ dancing ~~[crossed out]~~ leider-
hosen atop tables and drink to their
prowess — swallowing ~~[crossed out]~~ ~~[crossed out]~~ of beer —
(to accomodate , and, festively

redo

Untitled
September, 1996 – January, 1997
[MSS 0587   34   3]

My hips hurt.
Plus ankles (sp).

Dec. 19th —
up at 5 — sore — find it's
hard to walk.

* 11 am — Paul phones: would meet
tonight — will call circa 5, to set
time.

*   (I go to the bank. Buy
      a bottle of water (for ..
*   tomorrow), and a digital
      alarm clock (I hate.)
*   (I've already

We meet at Cantas at 6³⁰
eaten at Tub Siam): share two
margaritas ... Paul pays:
tells me I was 'not in good
shape' at Guy's reading; I'd
'had a few': evidently (according
to Paul) had interrupted the
reading with voiced comments,
that I had sat on the chair
in Doug's office and that Doug
(contrary to my perception) was
indeed present in the audience.

I, in fact, did not sit on a
chair in Doug's office, but

Untitled
January – February, 1997
[MSS 0587   35   1]

Crosson: Data #1
maxell®
MINI-FLOPPY DISK
(—from Paul.
(date?)

Untitled
February–October, 1997
[MSS 0587   35   2]

March 5 — Wednesday —

up at six —
Sort bills, balance, bank statement:
and commence:

* ☞ 1-800·441·5511 —

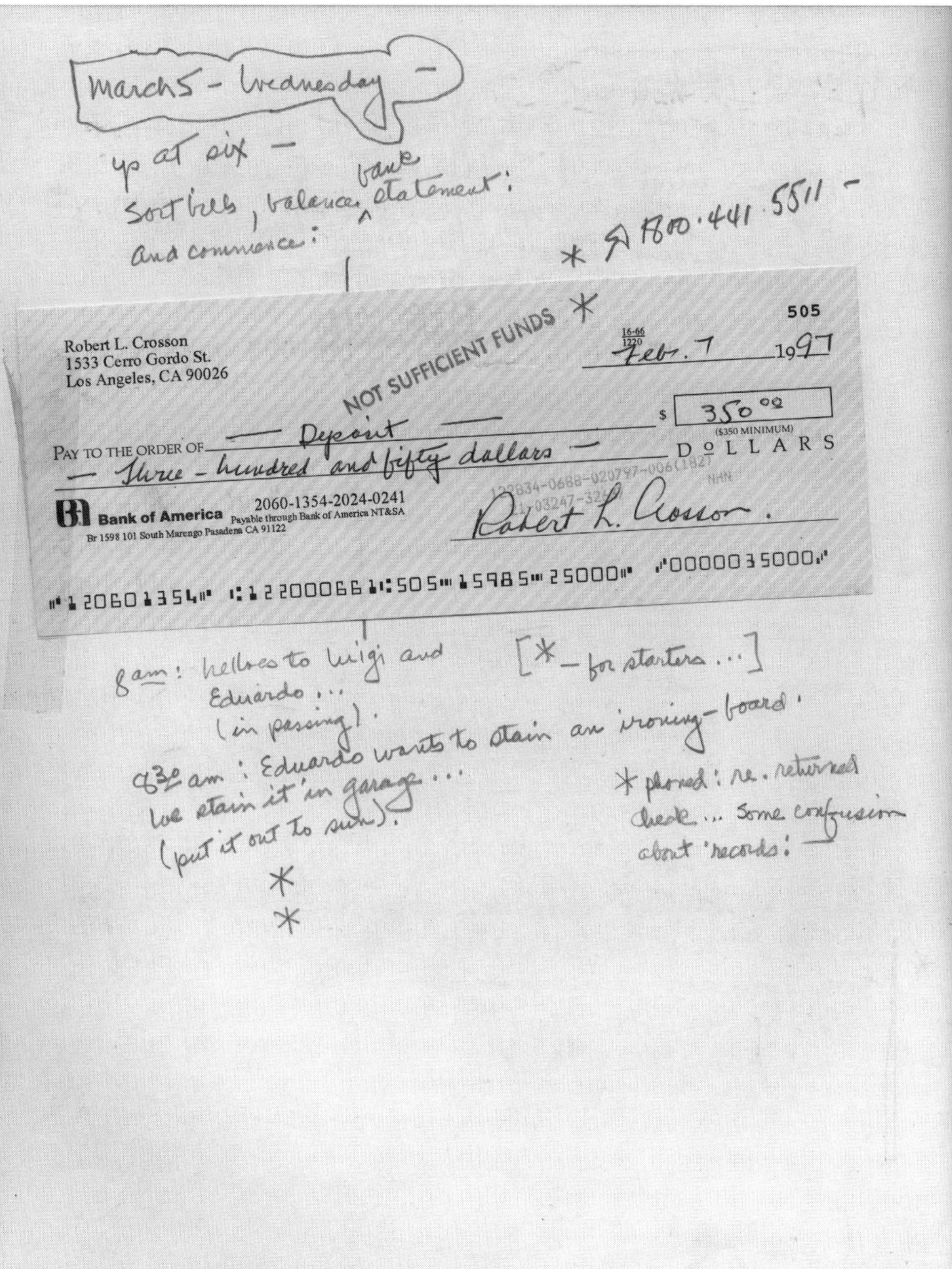

8 am: helloes to Luigi and   [* — for starters …]
       Eduardo …
       (in passing).
9 30 am : Eduardo wants to stain an ironing-board·
       We stain it in garage …   * phoned: re. returned
       (put it out to sun).   check … Some confusion
                                           about 'records:

          *
          *

Untitled
October, 1997 – March 3, 1998
[MSS 0587   35   3]

washrags
shorts
T-shirts
socks
+ SHOES.
(+ insoles)

2^{30} am – : a light drizzle.

martha (playful bitchery):
"He's like a girl on that telephone."

Up at seven. ~~morning light~~ (same light rain); some wind.
bed at nine. ▷ shit / eat jogurt.
up at 10^{30}.
rain seems to have stopped: quite chill.

?? ~~Seeing friends~~

"The Assumption is ~~an~~ not an
assumption!" — a friend.

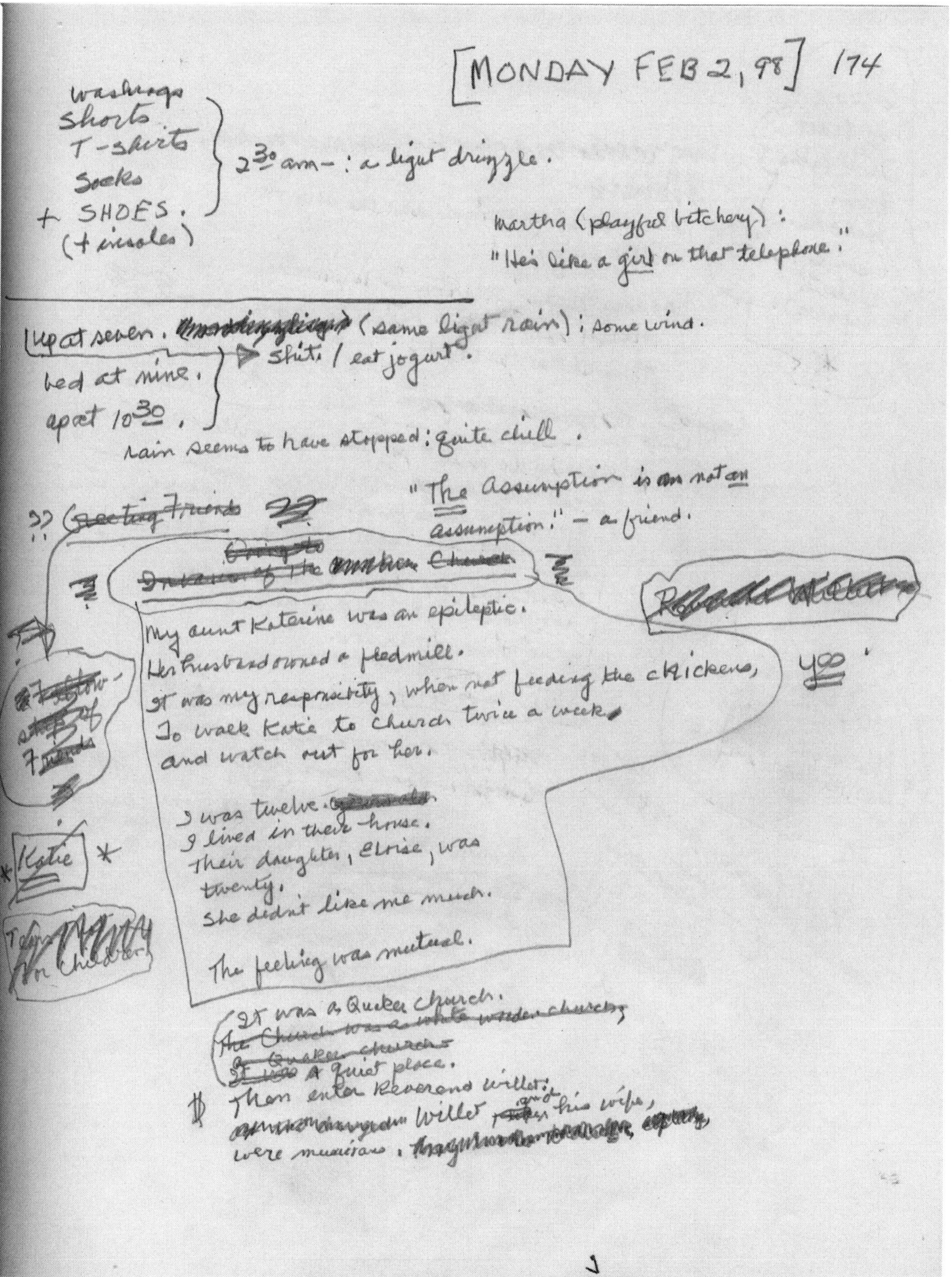

My aunt Katerine was an epileptic.
Her husband owned a feedmill.
It was my responsibility, when not feeding the chickens,
To walk Katie to church twice a week
and watch out for her.

I was twelve.
I lived in their house.
Their daughter, Eloise, was twenty.
She didn't like me much.

The feeling was mutual.

It was a Quaker church.
~~The Church was a white wooden church~~
~~a Quaker church~~
~~It was~~ A quiet place.
Then enter Reverend Willet:
~~...~~ Willet and his wife,
were musicians,

* Katie *

Untitled
March – July, 1998
[MSS 0587   36   1]

Announcing the College of Neglected Science's yet unnamed magazine project; in addition to the College's annual publication RIBOT.

By the <u>first of each month</u>, starting May 1998 and finishing April 1999, you will be asked to have 25 copies of 1-2 pages of your choosing arrive at:
    1533 Cerro Gordo St., Los Angeles, CA 90026.

The only limit on format and presentation is a left margin of <u>no less than 1.5 inches</u>.

Each month, as close to the first as possible, you will receive one copy of the publication: one year, twelve numbers. After the completion of the project, a selection (of at least 112 pages) will be made from the twelve numbers to run in RIBOT 7.

George Albon
Guy Bennett
Franklin Bruno
Avery Burns
Jeff Clark
Norma Cole
Robert Crosson
Jacques Debrot
Ray DiPalma
Barbara Guest
John Lowther
Douglas Messerli
Dennis Phillips
Chris Reiner
Martha Ronk
Leslie Scalapino
Standard Schaefer
Aaron Shurin
Paul Vangelisti
Catherine Wagner
Diane Ward

If you need further information, you may contact me at 213-662-4666 or pvangel@earthlink.net. Thanks very much for your interest and participation.

Paul Vangelisti

Untitled
July – December, 1998
[MSS 0587   36   2]

across road
(½ block down):

Sept 30th 98. Wednesday September
30th
↓ Yom Kippur

* BATHE

a cold morning —
after - breakfast "shower" (given by
pretty Mary) — clean shorts and
socks. (!!)

THE BAD SEED

(p. 16 - 20. "Killer Kids - reviewed by
by William   Joyce Carol Oates:
Match), with
an intro. by   NYRB - Nov. 6, 97.)
Elaine Showalter.

[childhood vs. "innocence"
↓
vs. MYTHO-
POETIC.]

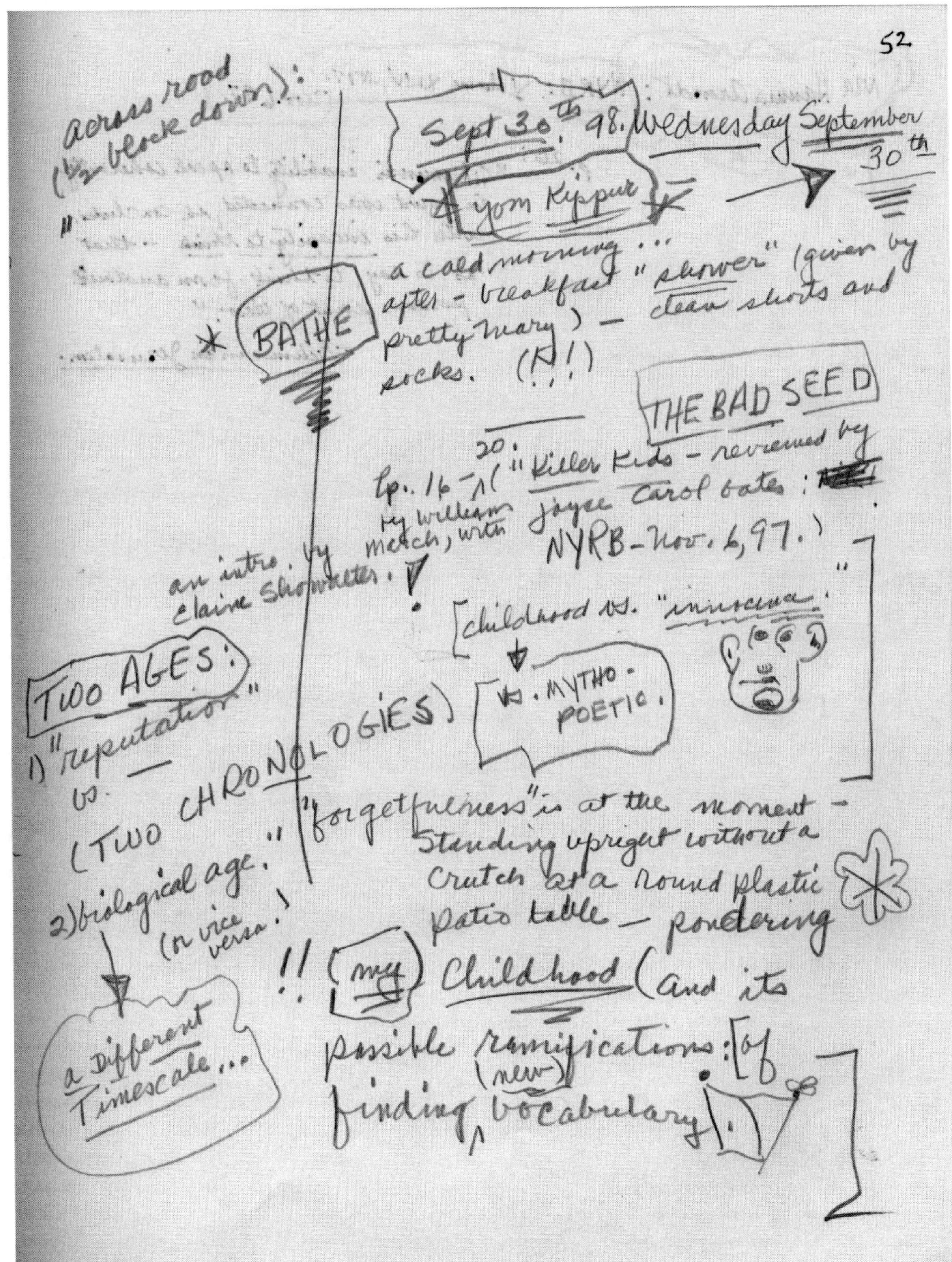

TWO AGES:
1) "reputation"
vs. —
(TWO CHRONOLOGIES)
2) biological age.
(or vice versa)

a different
Timescale ...

"forgetfulness" is at the moment —
standing upright without a
crutch at a round plastic
patio table — pondering
!! (my) Childhood (and its
possible ramifications: [of
(new)
finding vocabulary!.

Untitled
December, 1998
[MSS 0587   36   3]

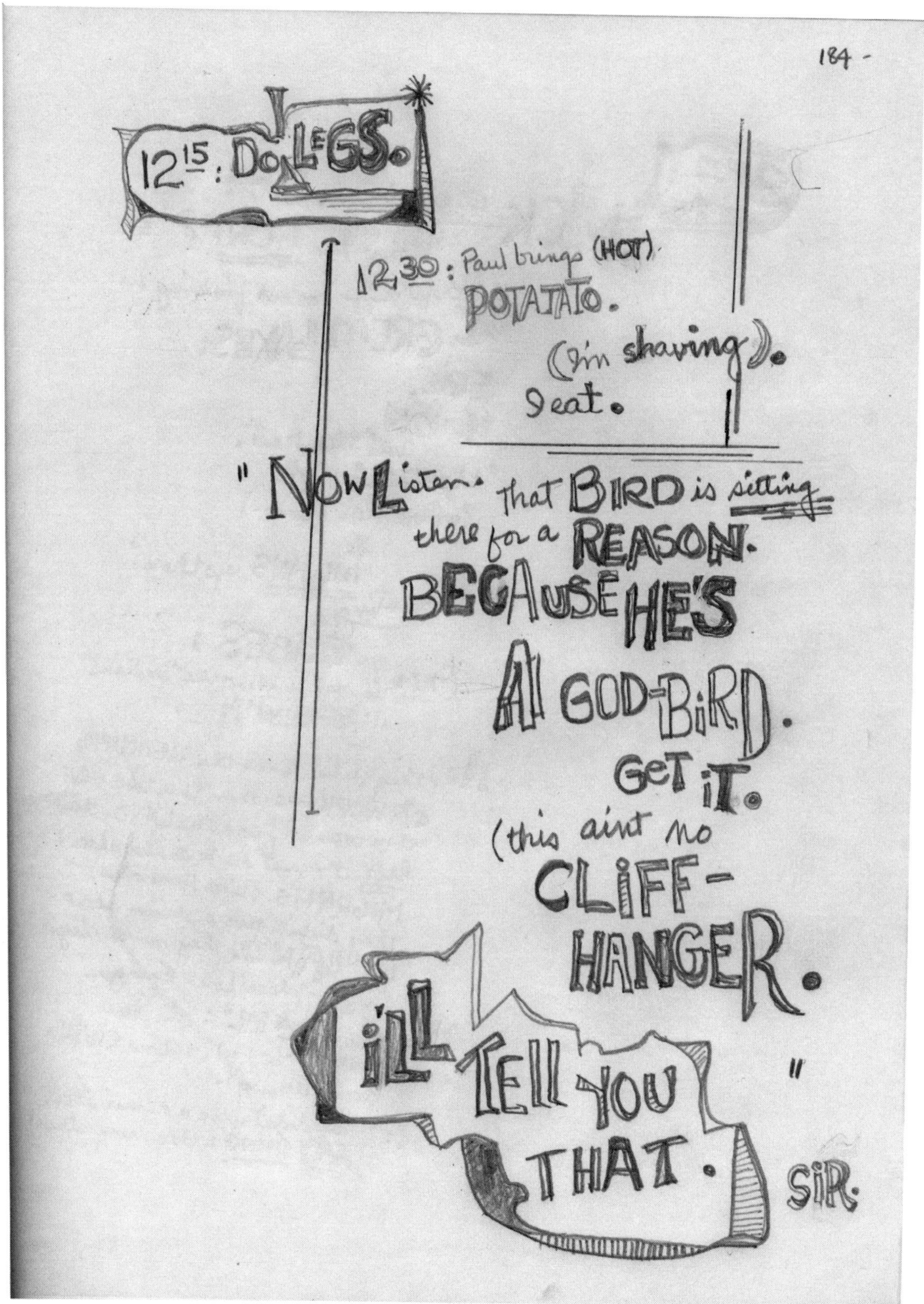

12¹⁵. Do LEGS.
12,30 : Paul brings (HOT)
POTATATO.
(I'm shaving).
I eat.
"NOW Listen. that BIRD is sitting there for a REASON. BECAUSE HE'S A GOD-BiRD. GET iT. (this aint no CLIFF-HANGER. iLL TELL YOU THAT. SiR. "

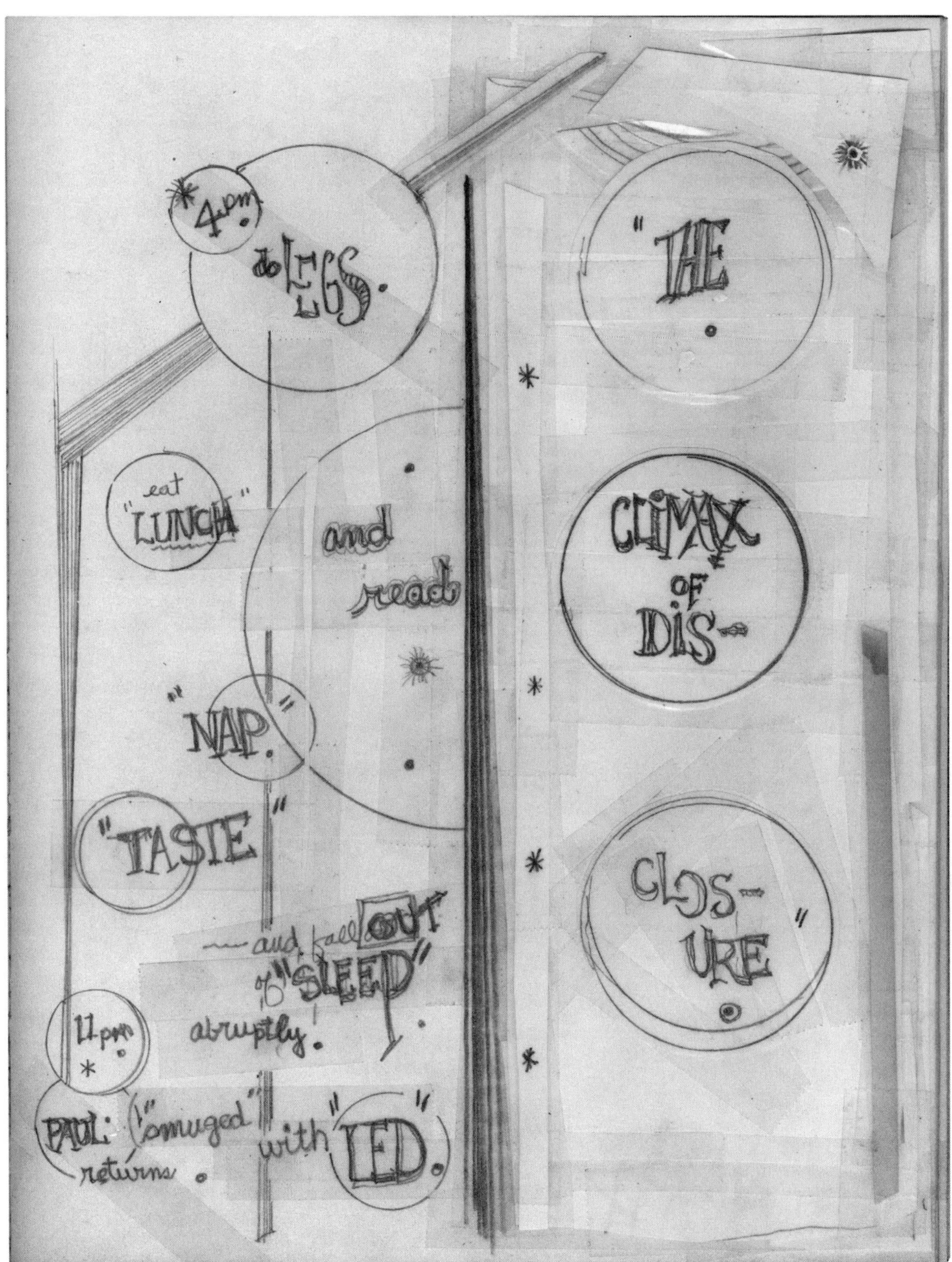
4 pm
to LEGS.
"eat LUNCH"
and read
"NAP."
"TASTE"
—— and fall OUT of "SLEEP" abruptly.
11 pm
PAUL: ("smuged") returns.
with "LED".
"THE
CLIMAX OF DIS—
CLOS— URE"

Untitled
February, 1999
[MSS 0587 37 2]

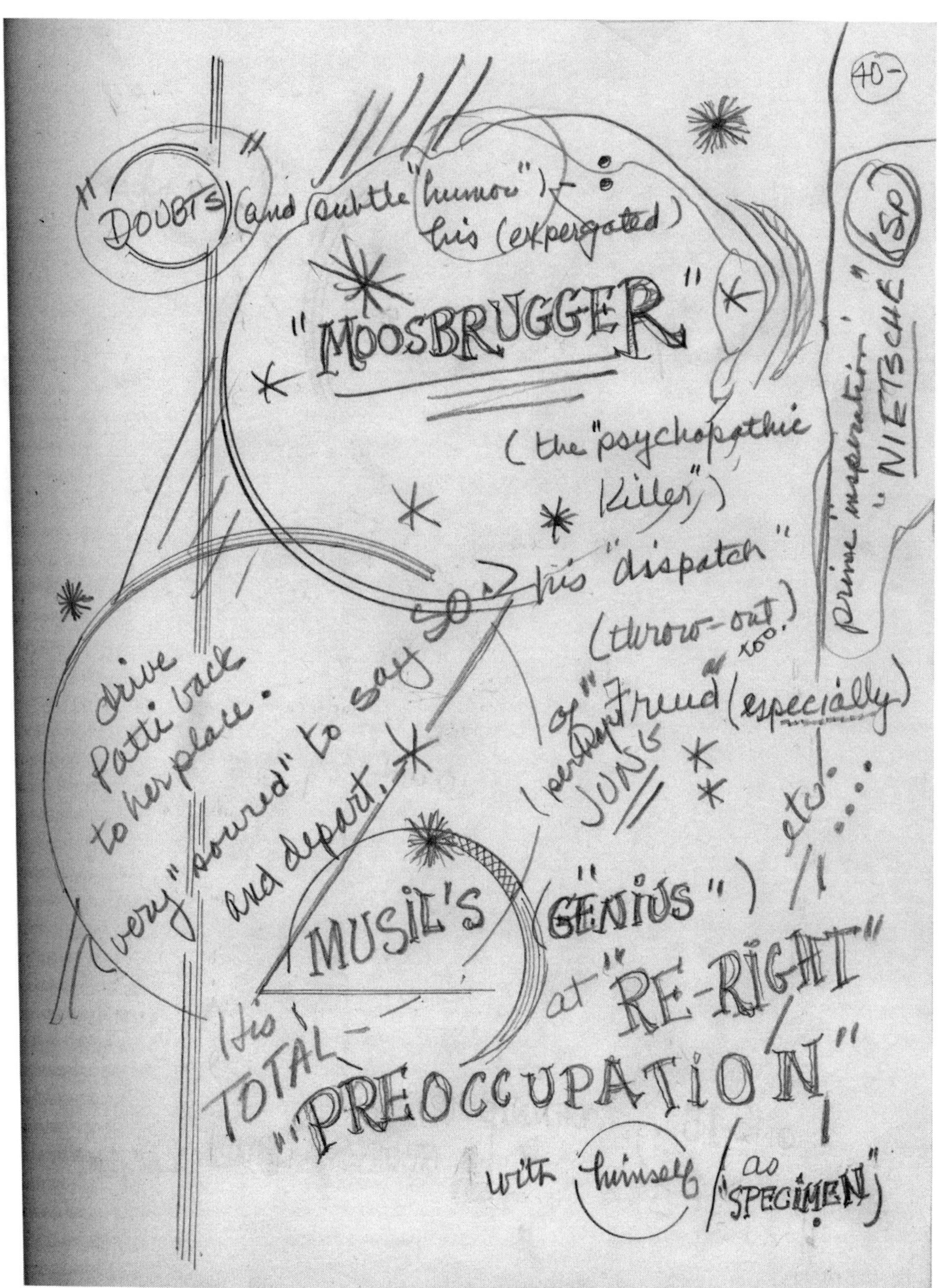
40-
"DOUBTS" (and subtle "humor") —
his (expurgated)
"MOOSBRUGGER"
(the "psychopathic Killer")
his "dispatch"
(throw-out)
of "Freud (especially)
JUNG etc . . .
prime inspiration "NIETSCHE" (sp)
drive Patti back to her place. very "soured" to say so and depart.
MUSIL'S ("GENIUS")
His TOTAL at "RE-RIGHT" PREOCCUPATION
with himself (as SPECIMEN)

Untitled
March, 1999
[MSS 0587   37   3]

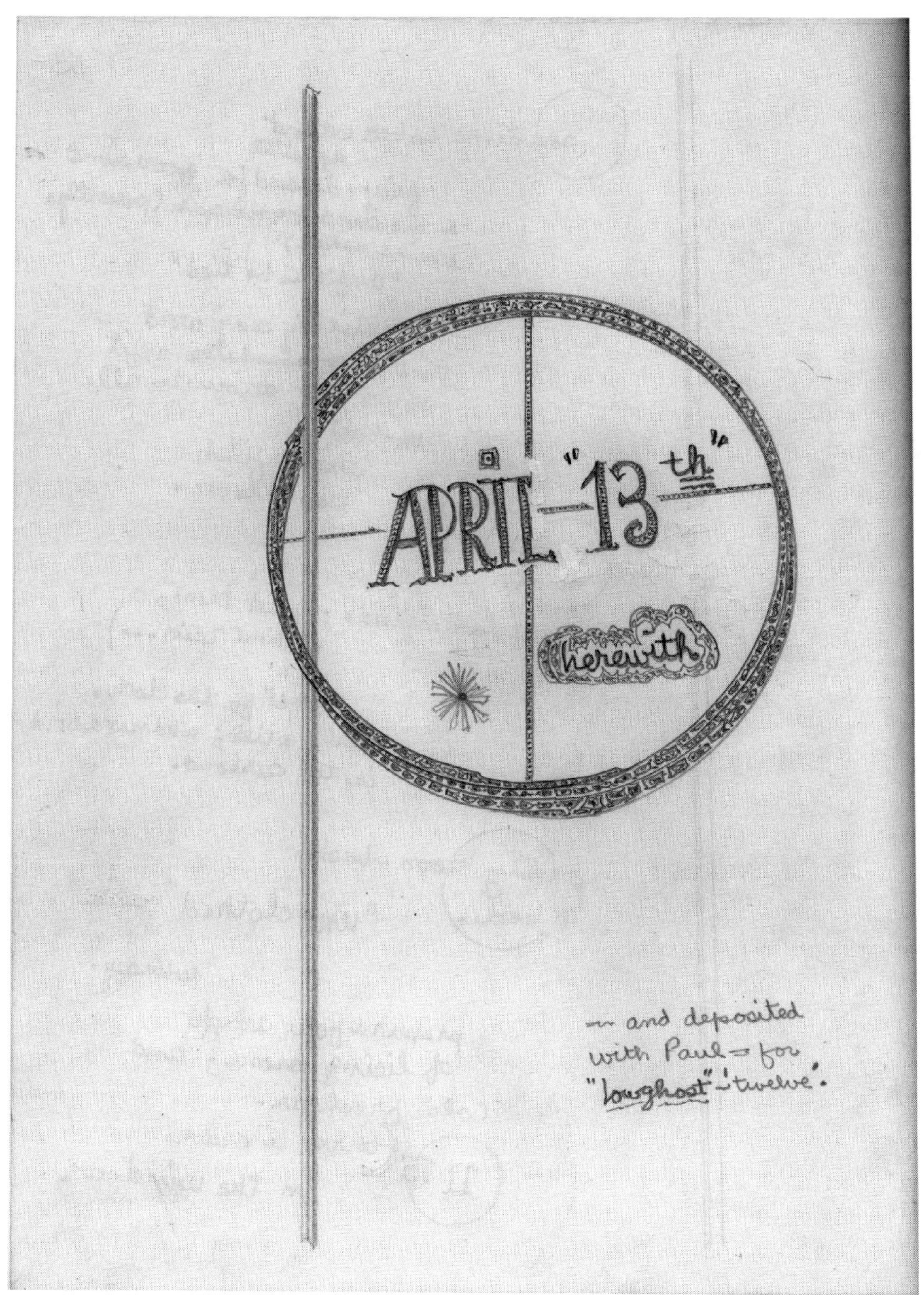

— and deposited
with Paul — for
"loughost"—twelve".

Untitled
May, 1999
[MSS 0587 38 1]

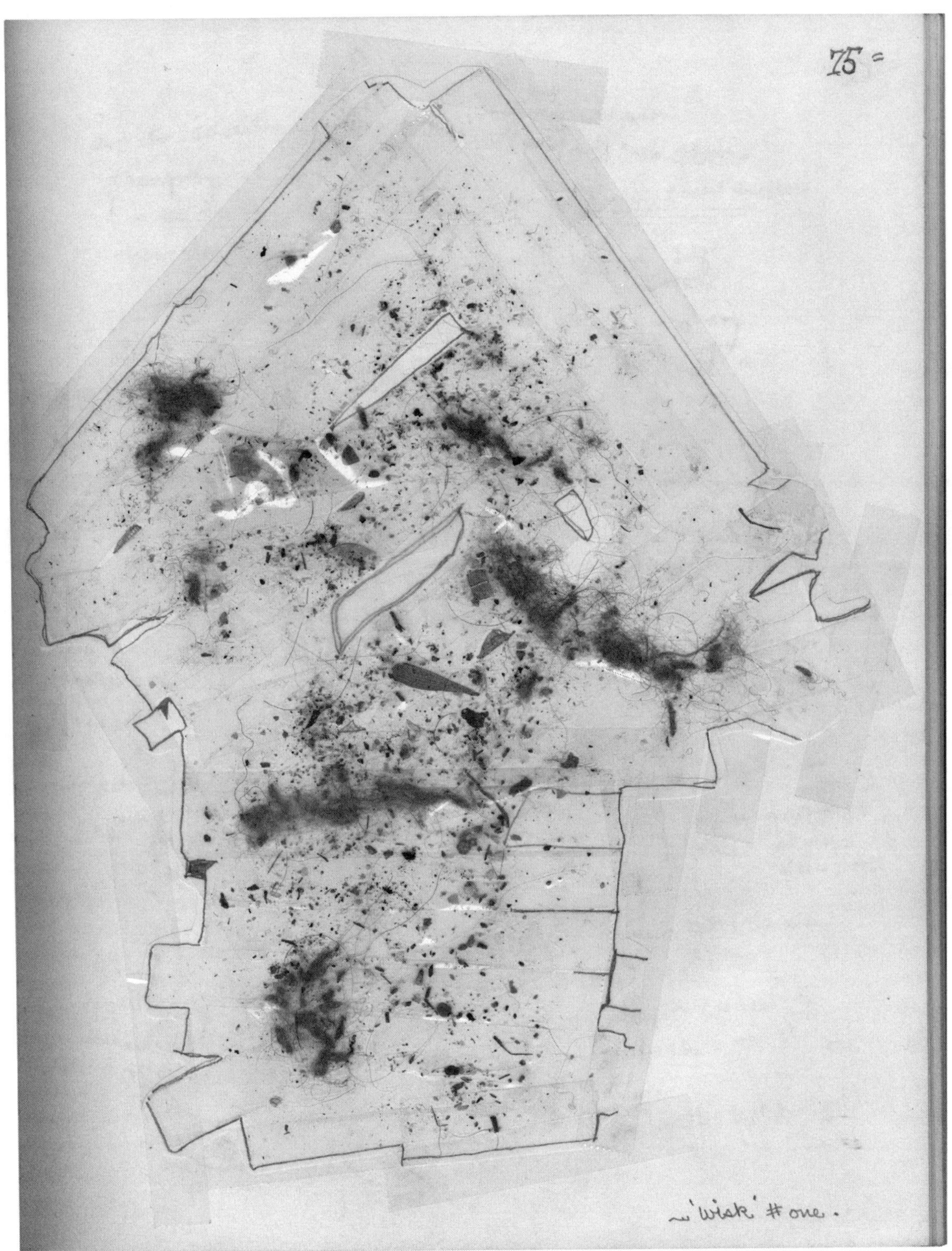
~ 'wisk' # one .

to stop smoking "(35$ the carton!)—" here's my chance—".

4:30 pm.
— eat.
3 AM — to bed.

— now, shall reread: 'to-Zack', maybe type 'it.
—if appropriate.
(—and do.

MONDAY   JULY 5th

("summary")

8:30 PM

point:
my whole-'nation' of 'a
letter to Bob'— was, a
mistake (I have, now,
tossed 'it out):

#1: my 'facts'—as re.
Bob's 'association'—with
Jack Miles — (as I dis-
covered (just now)—at
dinner-table— were
(are) totally wrong:
Zack & Miles were
NOT co-editors at
Cal-Press.
#2: I, of late (?)

~ would seem, essentially,
the same day (which, in
fact, 'it is': being ('in-
the-workplace') a three-
day holiday. *

∴ tonight celebrated with
a (splendid) dinner
(at Paul's); prepared
by Margosha — who
also (to me, charmingly)
"presided."

10:15 pm —

Margosha (in her car)
and Paul (in his) depart.
(minutes later, Paul
returns.
to his place.

over ▶ (by extension,) ▶

Untitled
July–August, 1999
[MSS 0587   38   3]

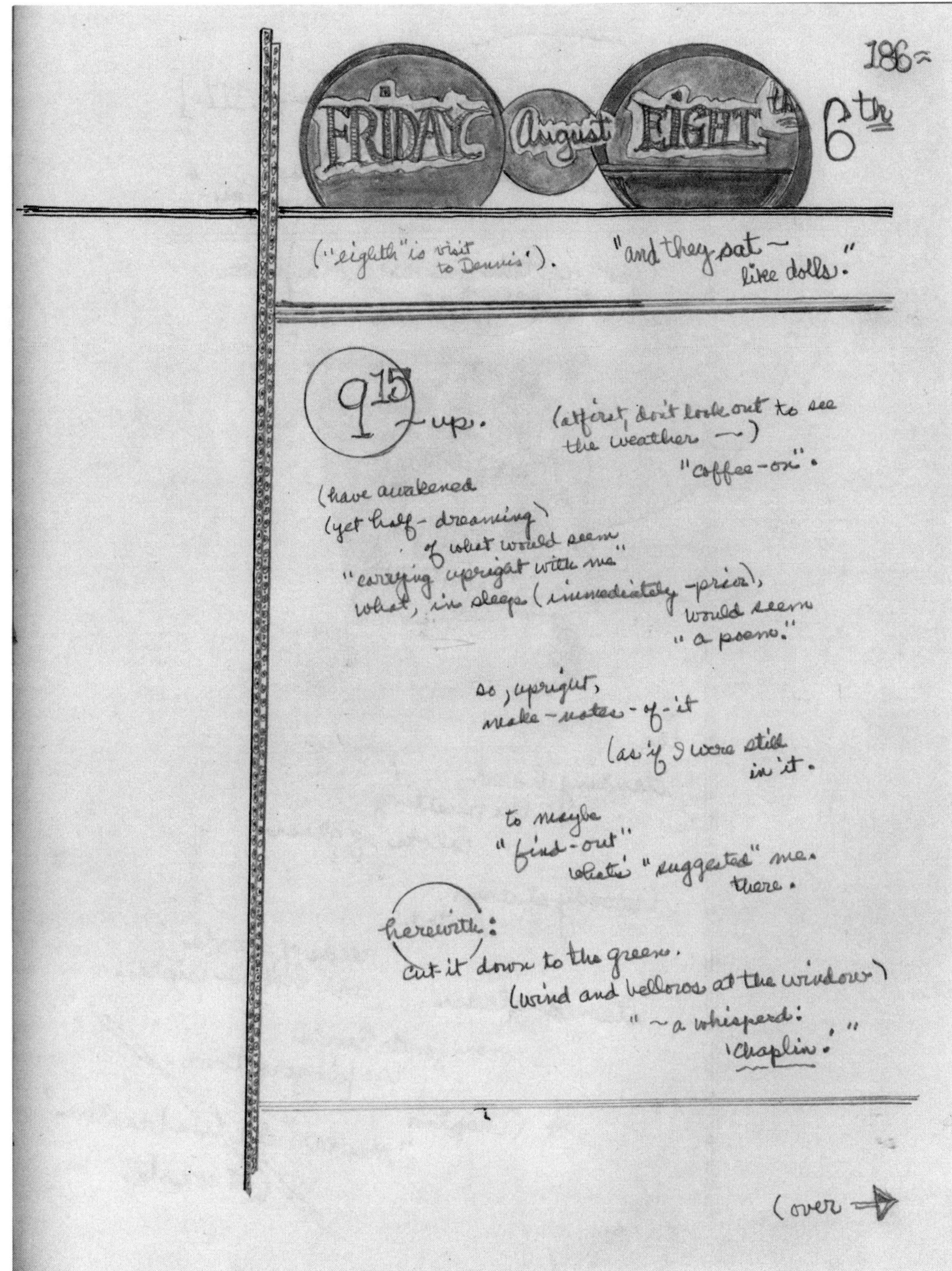

("eighth" is visit
  to Dennis').   "and they sat ~
                       like dolls."

9:15 up.   (at first, don't look out to see
                    the weather ~)
                         "coffee-on".

(have awakened
(yet half-dreaming)
      of what would seem.
  "carrying upright with me
  what, in sleep (immediately-prior),
                         would seem
                           "a poem."

              so, upright,
              make-notes-of-it
                    (as if I were still
                            in it.

              to maybe
              "find-out"
                  what's "suggested" me.
                       there.

herewith:
  cut it down to the green.
            (wind and bellows at the window)
                  " ~ a whispered:
                       'chaplin.'"

(over ⟹

Untitled
August, 1999
[MSS 0587 39 1]

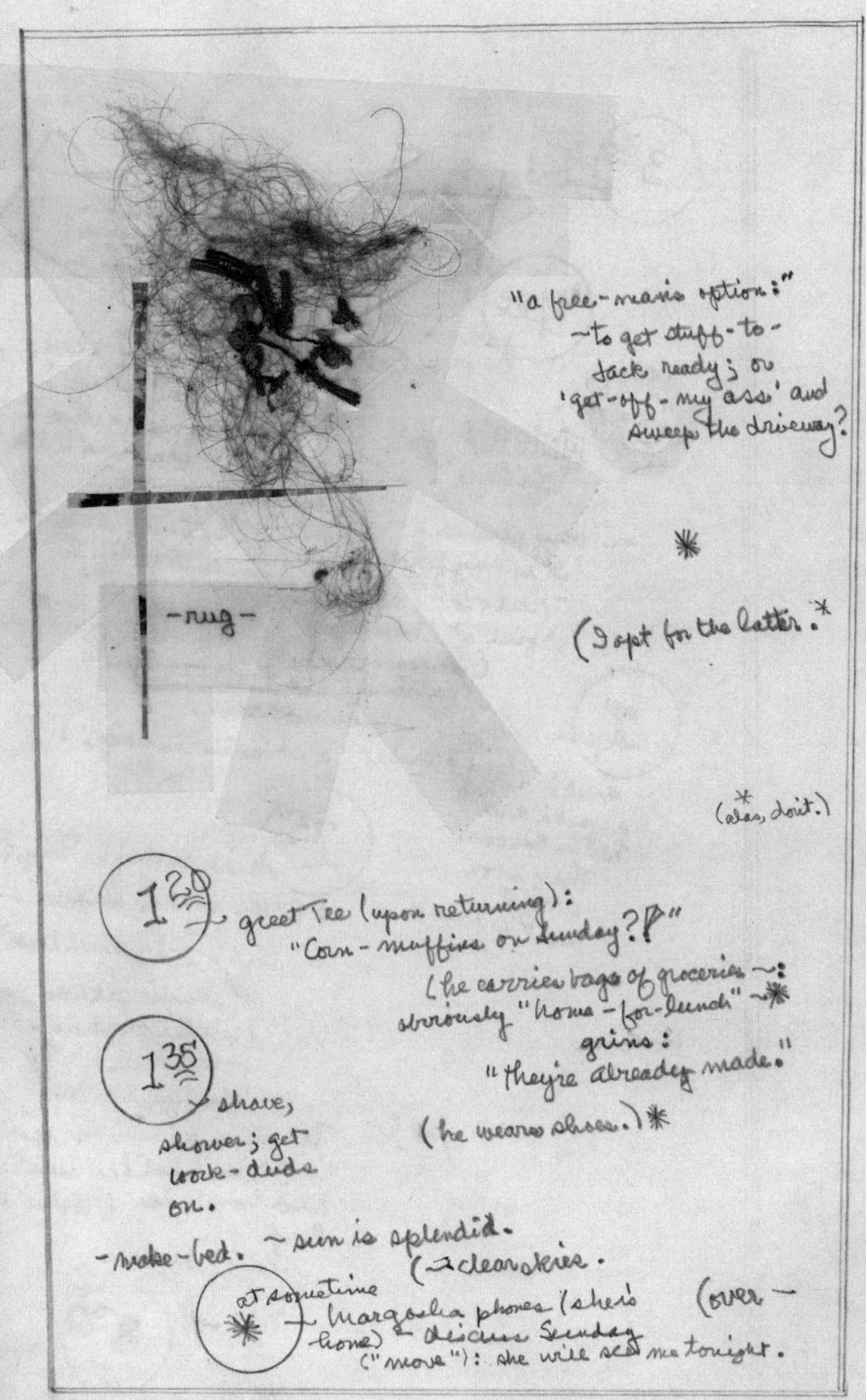

"a free-man's option:"
~ to get stuff - to -
tack ready; or
'get - off - my ass' and
sweep the driveway?

*

(I opt for the latter. *

*
(alas, don't.)

1²⁰ greet Tee (upon returning):
     "Corn - muffins on Sunday?♭"

           (he carries bags of groceries ~:
           obviously "home - for - lunch" *
                      grins:
                 " they're already made."

           (he wears shoes.) *

1³⁵ shave,
     shower; get
     work - duds
     on.

- make - bed. ~ sun is splendid.
                  (~ clear skies.
        at sometime
     * ~ Margosha phones (she's   (over -
        home) ~ discuss Sunday
        ("move"): she will see me tonight.

Untitled
September, 1999
[MSS 0587   39   2]

Monday Sept. 13th.

(Jim Bridges ~ a reminder ~:
"Remember ~ your 'face', on the screen,
is three - hundred times bigger ~ ."
                    - than it is!

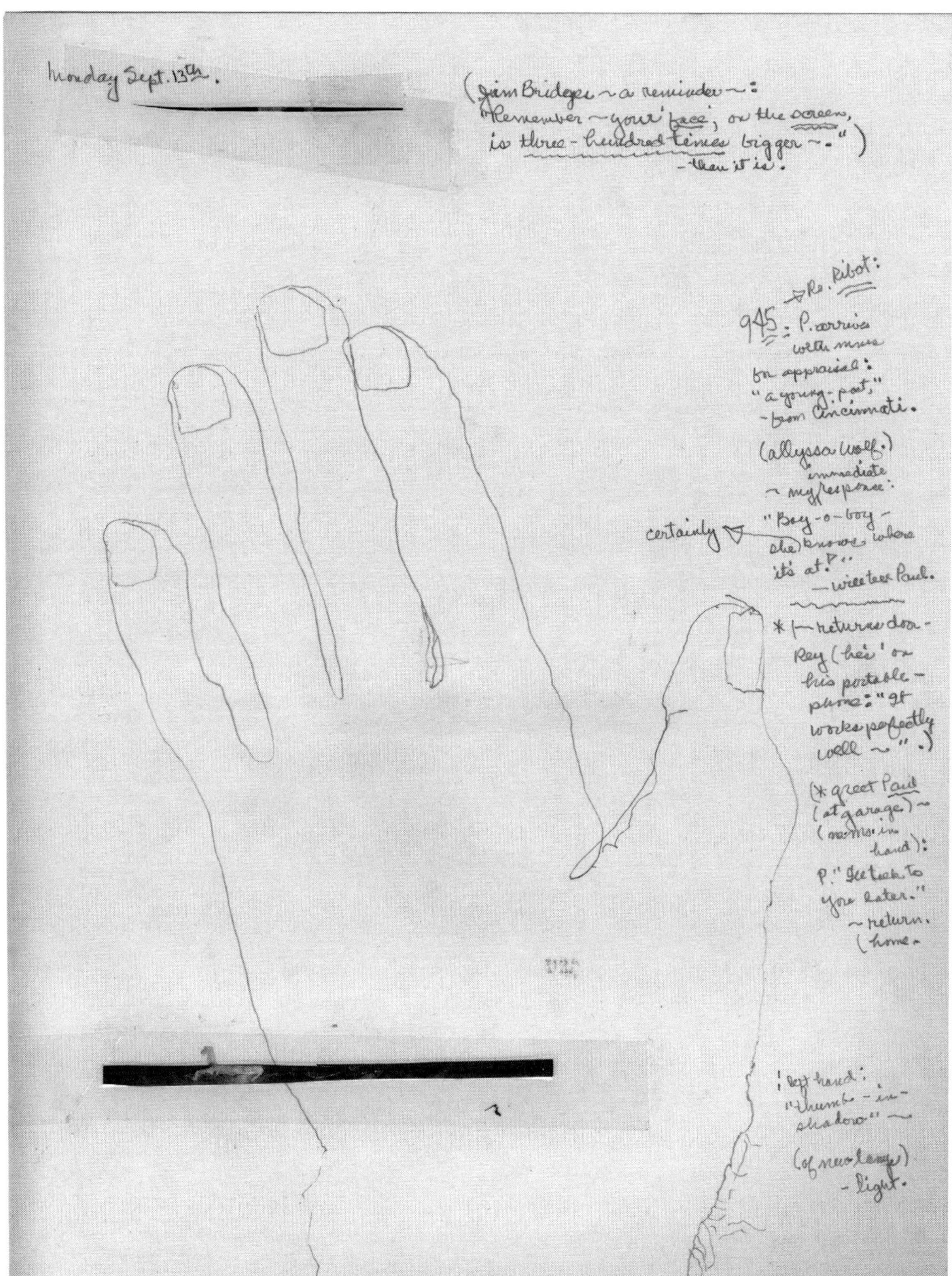

→ Re. Ribot:
9^45 : P. arrives
    with mss
for appraisal:
"a young - poet,"
- from Cincinnati.

(Allyssa Wolf.)
        immediate
~ my response:

"Boy - o - boy -
she knows where
it's at!" ..
        - writes Paul.

certainly ▷

* |— returns door-
key ('he' on
his portable -
phone: "It
works perfectly
well ~ ".)

(* greet Paul
(at garage) ~
(mss. in
        hand):
P.:" I'll talk to
you later."
        ~ return.
        (home -

: left hand:
"thumb - in -
shadow" ~

(of new lamp)
        - light.

Untitled
October, 1999
[MSS 0587   39   3]

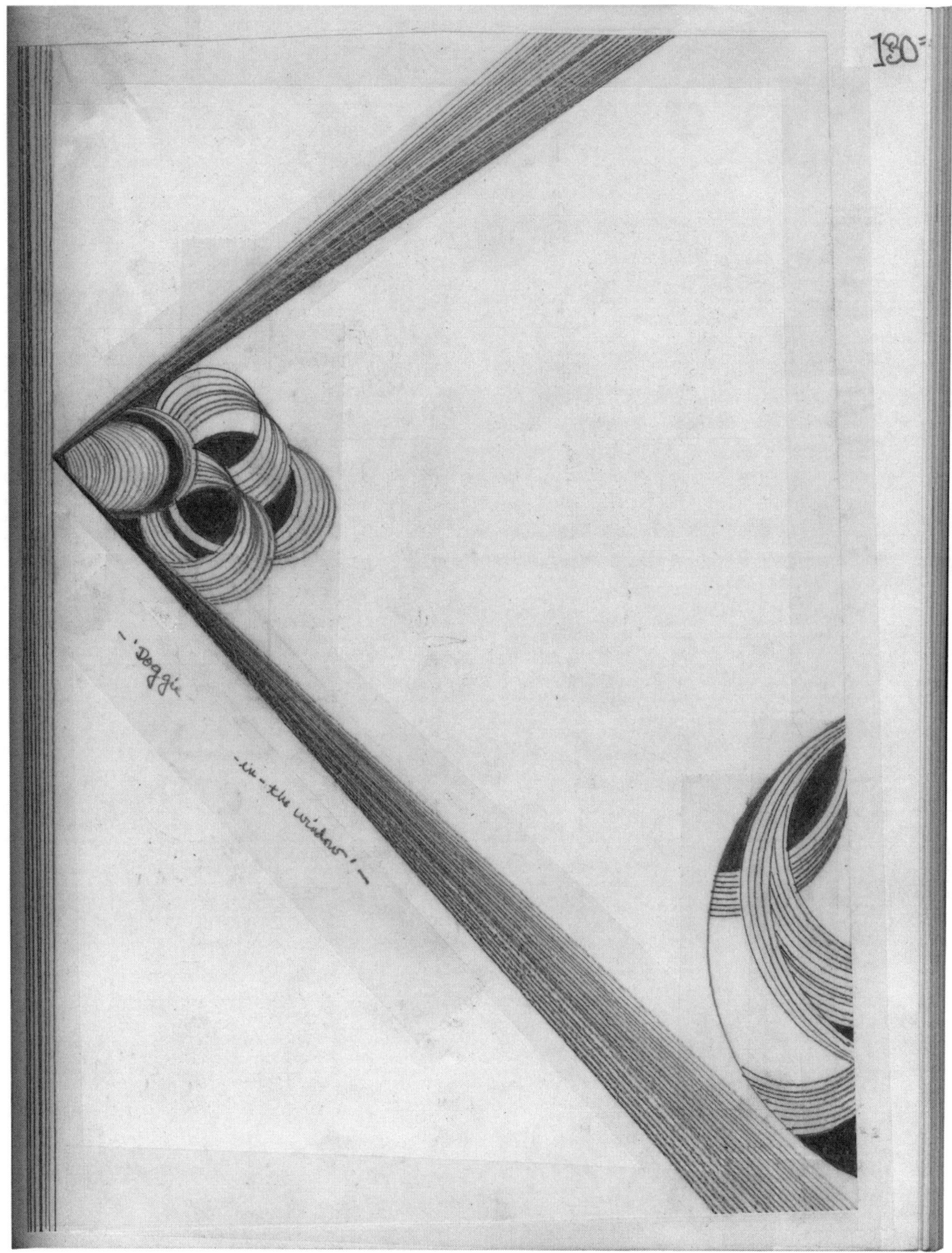
- "Doggie
- in - the window! -

Untitled
November, 1999
[MSS 0587   39   4]

"Collages"   (presently – as of 12.22.99): (plus 2 "pencil drawings"
                                                 plus 2 "pencil+ink"):

'Paul-piece' ('review')(small)   (another -'small'*)
'Grinberg'   2 (very small)
'Wrestler'
'photo-graph'
"reflection #2." (pencil)   'Margosa-piece' (the one
'humility' (pencil)   she likes)
'Masque' (pen & pencil)   "Mosque"
'the shining') " " "   "specimen-notes" (early)
"He" (collage)   "'Art' was this fireman
"no promises" "   I knew."
'circus of Dr. Lao' (collage)   'Piano-player'
'chekov's tree' "   'avenue'
the 'landing field' "   'a pretty young girl'
'Katyinpammer'   'family' (lorri has) *
'study #3'   'my cat likes me'
'landmark'   'filibuster'
'ein cormischa weltstraum #2'   'Schimm' (the first
'niagra'   *   collage ~)
'untitled' (of 'outside'-collage)
'Helmutt'   * (seventeen 'little' pieces ~)
'post-card'   "David" (collage)
'nite-out' (b & white collage).   'couture' "
'cinema'   ('for Dennis') "
'untitled'   'desert song' "
'Hurrah (for Anything)"   'what's new in the world' "
'boat'   "Untitled" "

House Organ
c/o Kenneth Warren
1250 Belle Avenue
Lakewood, Ohio 44107

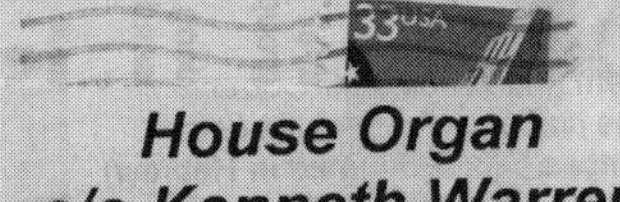

House Organ

Number 29 Winter 2000

Cid Corman

from: IMMEDIATE

Poetry is life —

every living moment —

now is death's poem.

***

There's so much to do

about doing nothing and

it takes a lifetime.

(* viz: 77+ volumes of
(ongoing) 'Dreybooks'.)

Untitled
February – March, 2000
[MSS 0587   40   2]

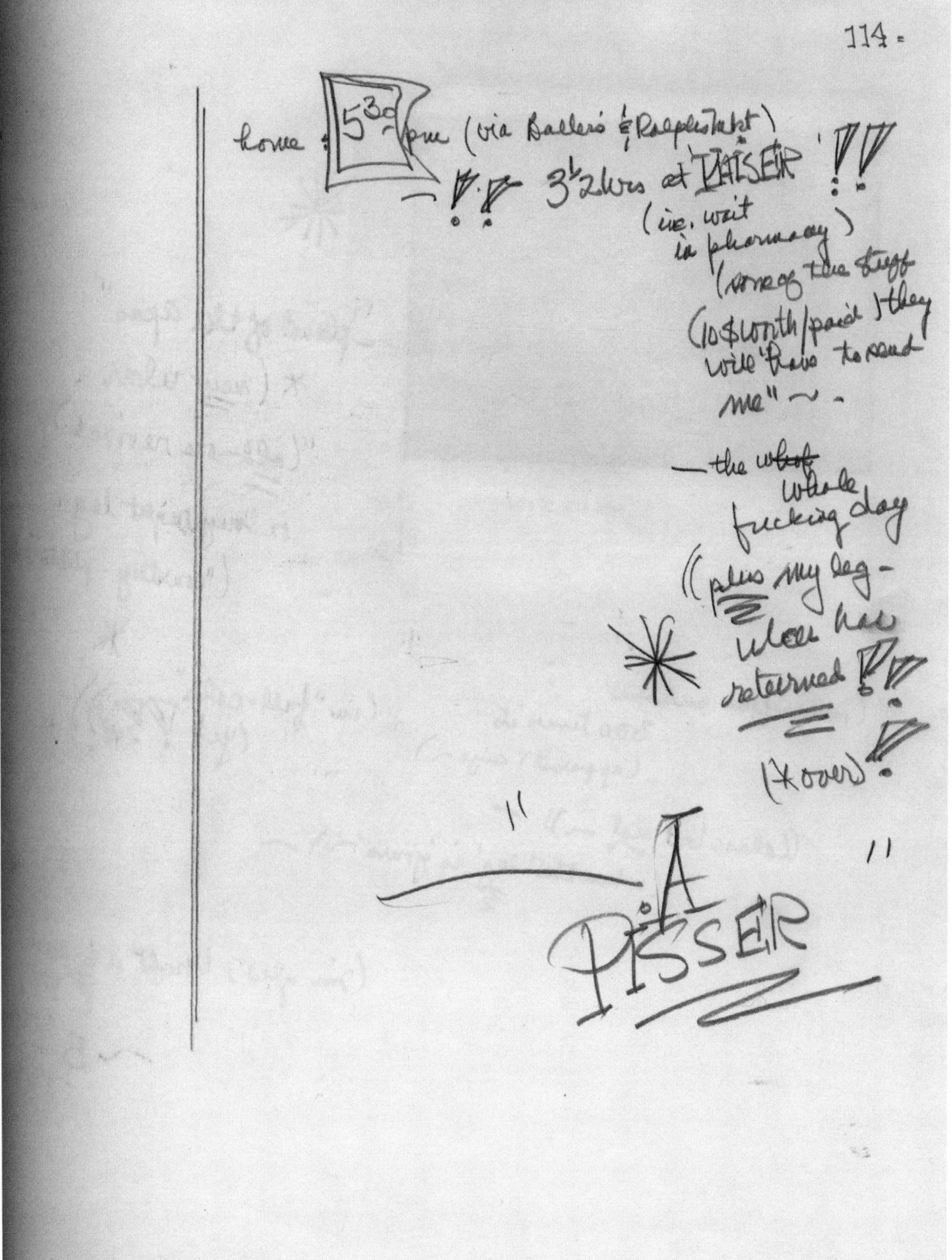
home : 5³⁰ pme (via Ballero & Ralphs Tckt)
!! 3½ hrs at 'KAISER' !!!
(ie. wait
in pharmacy)
(some of the stuff
(10$ month/paid) they
will 'have to send'
me" ~ -
— the whole
fucking day
((plus my leg -
ulcer has
returned !!!
(over)
"A
PISSER"

Untitled
April, 2000
[MSS 0587   40   3]

April 28:00
Friday   : rough - draft :

Dear Jim SVEJDA:

KUSC is the only station I listen to (especial applause XXX
for the new Antenna (sp?); _you_ (anytime); Bill McGlaughlin
(St. Paul Sunday); plus else...(I am a supporter of the
station (when I have the $),at the moment unable to con-
tribute.

I wonder(*I'm a 'published' poet)have you ever read Hector
Berlioz' 'EVENINGS IN THE ORCHESTRA' (a droll delight); and
2: (aside from much appreciating your 'attention' to
Charles Ives (any!): would you sometime play (to me a
'colossal-classic) Virgil Thompson's "4-Saints in 3-Acts:
SUPERB.

Many thanks for "being on the Planet: your fxx feet,
so soundly entrenched."

                         Sincerely,

————

P.S.: I am 71 years-old—presently 'a cripple':
yet horney for anyone (usually young) who 'would stand still
long enough'; as, for me, MUSIC always does.

My very best;

Robert Crowon.

:An eccentric FAN of Alice B. Toklas, AKA Gertrude Stein....
Also (alas, a wretched typist.

                        bc.   "KUSC"
                                    tele# 213-514.1400
                                    address :
                                         P.O. Box 77913
                                         L.A. 90007-
                                                 0913.
                                 — (precisely): (6:30 pm

7:30 pm ~ whilst 'attending'
: Katt-olabs (Margliosa
insists (fearing further
infection of her it foot) she
needsbe here ~
~ and is .
                             (over)

        ← will phor 'tomorrow —

Untitled
May – July, 2000
[MSS 0587   41   1]

purple - flower above his left ear.

(— I like him, a little.) !! "we piss" together —)).

— at some point, have finished
'new' - collage; and have hung it
in bathroom — directly above
the "toilet". Splendid — !!

("Badenzimmer-Kunst-werke") :

— of course !!

((appropriately.)) —

9:30 PM : home
(with Paul) from "Casitas" —

; to bed : 10:20 PM :

(yet "turned - on"; (by the "new - bed")
and quite full.))) named:

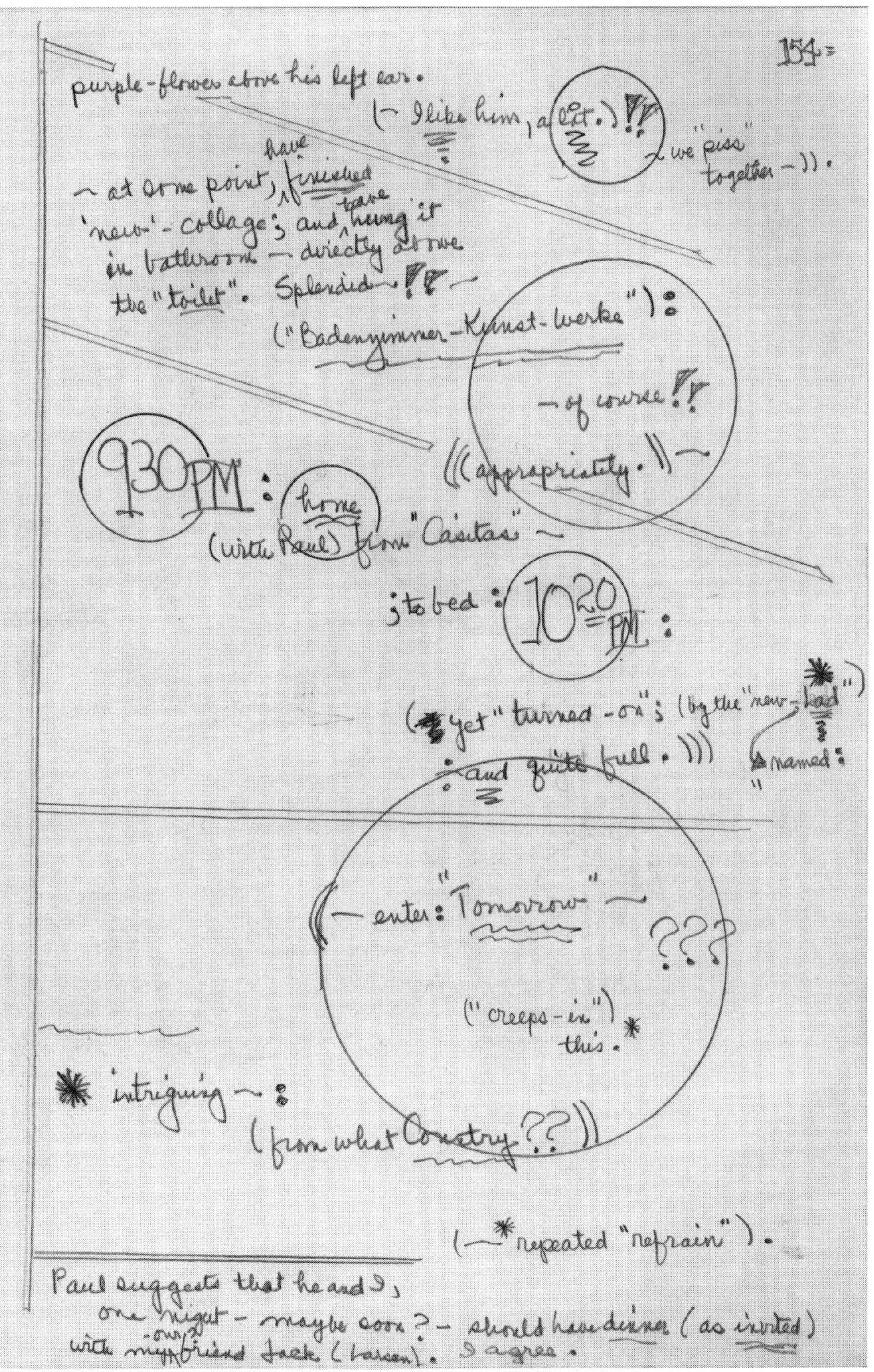

— enter: "Tomorrow" — ???

("creeps - in")
this.

intriguing — :
(from what Country ??))

(— repeated "refrain").

Paul suggests that he and I,
one night — maybe soon? — should have dinner (as invited)
with my friend Jack (Larsen). I agree.

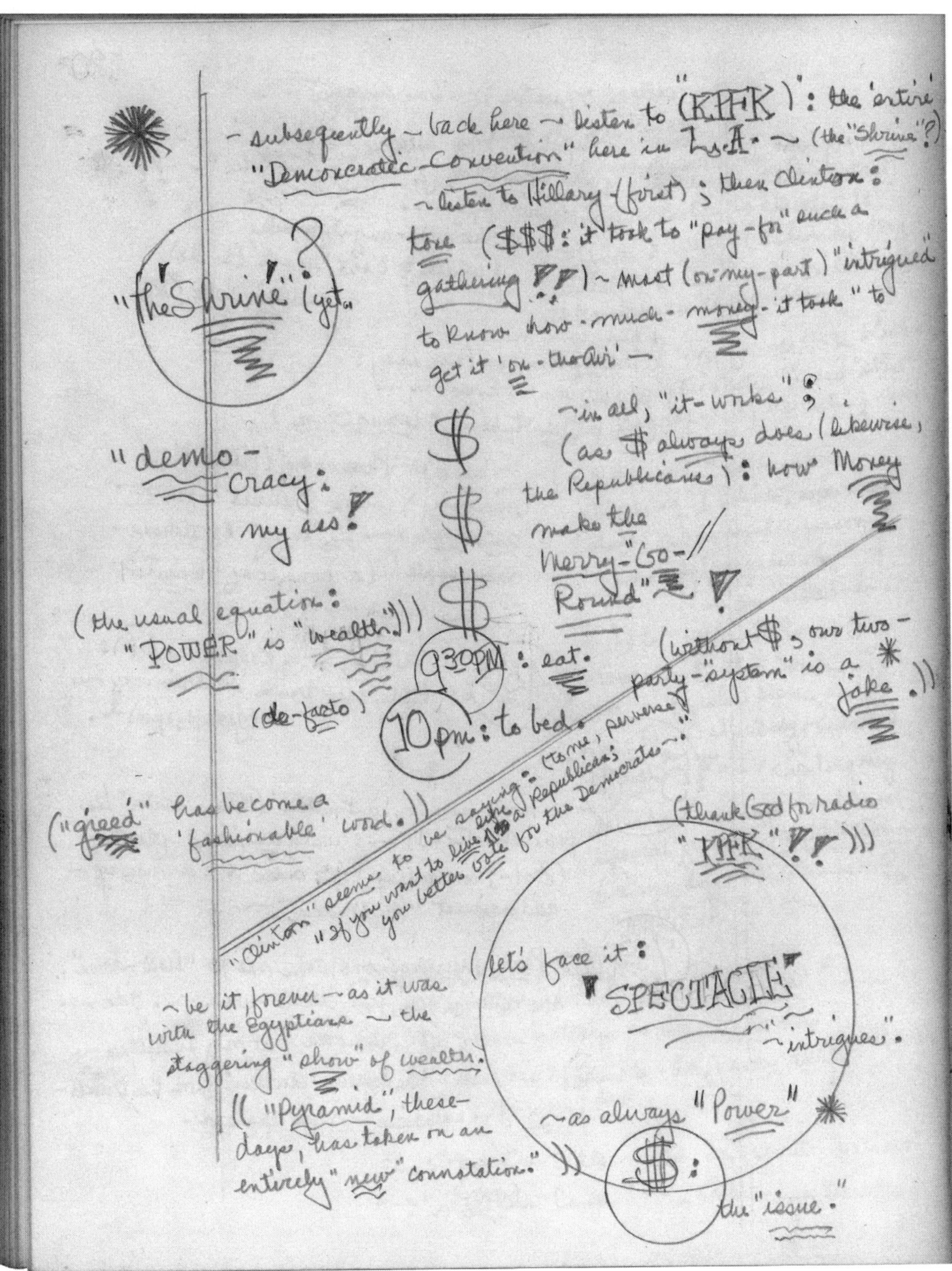

– subsequently – back here – listen to ("KPFK") : the 'entire'
"Democratic Convention" here in L.A. – (the "Shrine"?)
– listen to Hillary (first) ; then Clinton :
too ($$$: it took to "pay-for" such a
gathering ‼) – most (on-my-part) "intrigued"
to know how – much – money – it took " to
get it 'on-the-air' –

"the Shrine" (yet.

"demo –
cracy :
my ass!

(the usual equation :
"POWER" is "wealth.")))

(de-facto)

$

$

$ 9:30PM : eat.

10pm : to bed.

("greed" has become a
'fashionable' word.))

~ in all, "it – works" ?
(as $ always does (likewise,
the Republicans) : how Money
make the
Merry – "(Go –
Round" ‼

(without $; our two –
party – "system" is a
joke .))

"Clinton" seems to be saying : (to me, perverse
"if you want to live like a Republican;
you better vote for the Democrats.

(thank God for radio
"KPFK" ‼)))

~ be it forever – as it was
with the Egyptians – the
staggering "show" of wealth.

(("Pyramid", these –
days, has taken on an
entirely "new" connotation."

(let's face it :
SPECTACLE"
~ "intrigues".
~ as always "Power"
$:
the "issue."

Untitled
September – October, 2000
[MSS 0587   41   3]

"CANS": (previous notes):

City "pickup tel #'s":

    Sanitation Dept: 1-213-473-7878.

    (("Bulky-Item"-truck: 323-227-7334.))

       (Another#:-1531-33)∴??

    general Info: 1-800-773-2489

* our (present) black, trashcan #'s: (2):

    " OBI (ours) 4987 "

    " OBI ("Tee's) 47840 "

    (~ will be delivered "day-after-
        pickup")

        (on Thursdays):

    (and replaced with new-ones).

:·"empty"

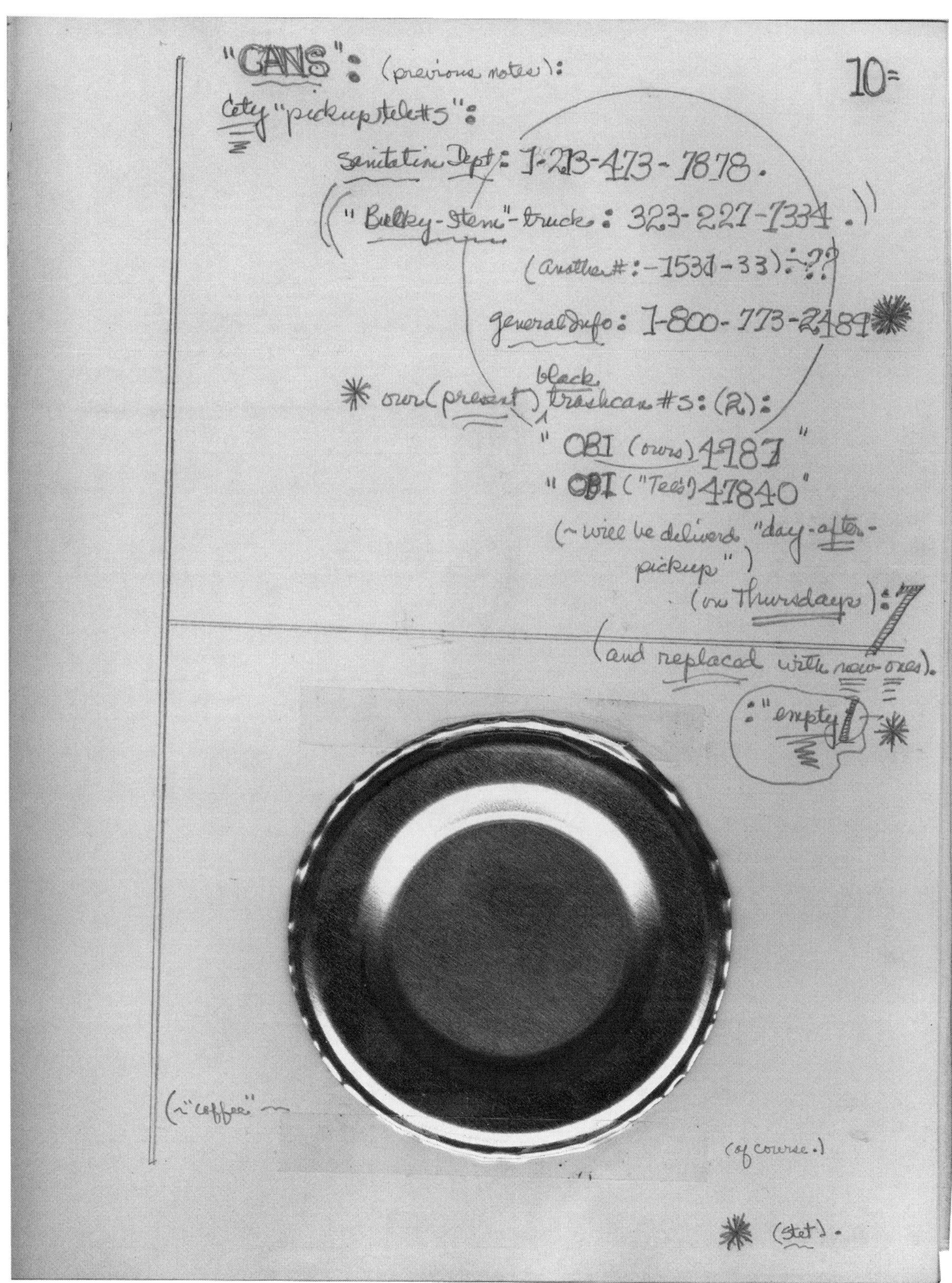

(~"coffee"

(of course.)

* (stet).

Untitled
October – December, 2000
[MSS 0587   42   1]

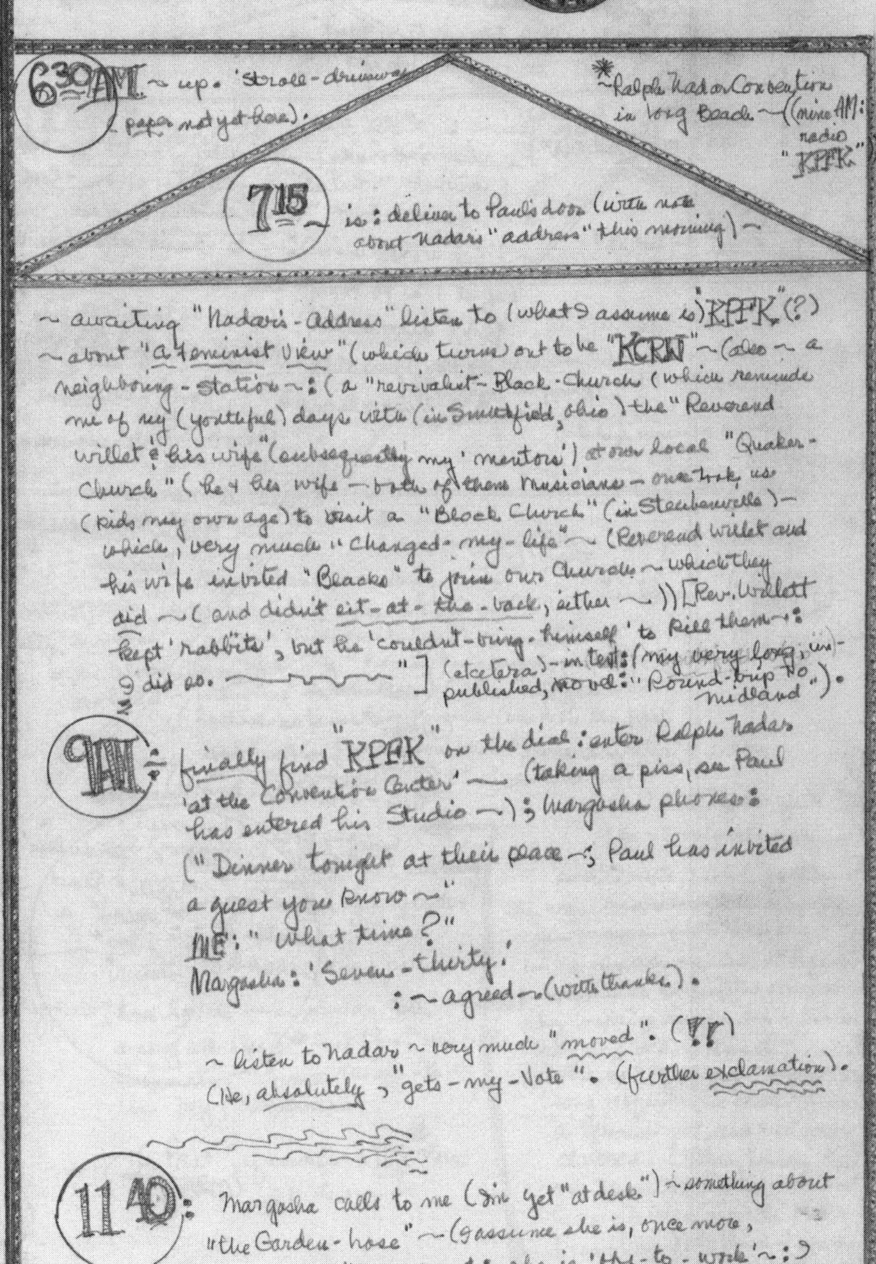

SUNDAY November 5

— clear skies; some sun.

6:30 AM ~ up. 'stroll - driveway (paper not yet here).

→ Ralph Nader Convention in Long Beach — (nine AM: radio "KPFK.")

7:15 is: deliver to Paul's door (with note about Nader's "address" this morning) ~

~ awaiting "Nader's - Address" listen to (what I assume is) "KPFK" (?) ~ about "a feminist view" (which turns out to be "KCRW" ~ (also ~ a neighboring - station ~: (a "revivalist - Black - Church (which reminds me of my (youthful) days with (in Smithfield, Ohio) the "Reverend Willet & his wife" (subsequently my 'mentors') at our local "Quaker - Church" (he & his wife - both of them musicians - once took us (kids my own age) to visit a "Black Church" (in Steubenville) ~ which, very much "changed - my - life" ~ (Reverend Willet and his wife invited "Blacks" to join our Church ~ which they did ~ (and didn't sit - at - the - back, either ~)) [Rev. Willet kept 'rabbits', but he 'couldn't-bring - himself' to kill them ~: I did so. ——————— "] (etcetera) - in text: (my very long, un-published, novel: "Round-trip to midland").

9 AM finally find "KPFK" on the dial: enter Ralph Nader 'at the Convention Center' ~ (taking a piss, so Paul has entered his Studio ~); Margosha phones:
("Dinner tonight at their place ~; Paul has invited a guest you know ~"
ME: "what time?"
Margosha: 'Seven - thirty.'
: ~ agreed ~ (with thanks).

~ listen to Nader ~ very much "moved". (!!)
(He, absolutely, "gets - my - Vote". (further exclamation).

11:40: Margosha calls to me (I'm yet "at desk") ~ something about "the Garden - hose" ~ (I assume she is, once more, "gardening" ~ but not: she is 'off - to - work' ~:) great her & she has brushed - the leaves from her car ~

(over →)

Untitled
December, 2000–February, 2001
[MSS 0587 42 2]

"ambiguity" wd seem 'forefront' — (my "recollection" of things)".
                            — as (viz): this —
                    a photo of myself and my brother
                                " — as "kids"
                        (in yesterday's — mail) — : ✳

Paul
informs
"plumbers" will
"re-install" new
"driveway - "plumbing"
(i.e. "drain"): for 800$.
            — I applaud . (?: Nick
            will "shit-a-turkey" ? ?? .

(in "Monigor, PA".)
            ?

(11:05): Margasha departs:
        (en route to visit her "optometrist" — to have
        "eyes-checked" for "new-glasses".))
                    —"alah" visits :
                        give her some milk .))
            ~ I depart — for Bank : 20$ cash :
            — get cigarettes, beer, and
                    $15 - gas .))

✳ viz ("apropos") today's letter from him :   (over : pg. 123.)

Untitled
February – April, 2001
[MSS 0587   42   3]

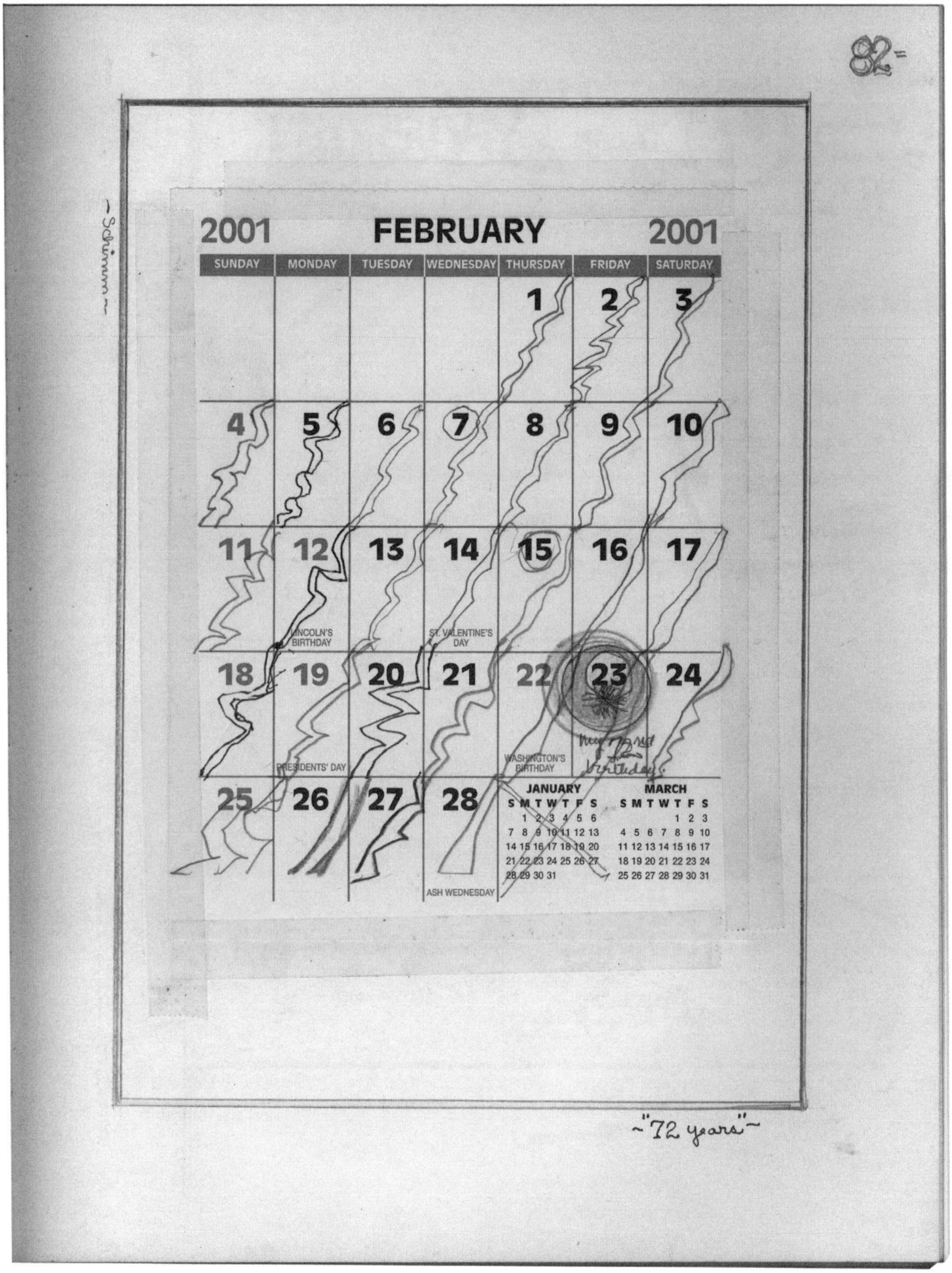

~ Schumm ~

2001   FEBRUARY   2001

SUNDAY | MONDAY | TUESDAY | WEDNESDAY | THURSDAY | FRIDAY | SATURDAY

1 2 3
4 5 6 7 8 9 10
11 12 13 14 15 16 17
18 19 20 21 22 23 24
25 26 27 28

LINCOLN'S BIRTHDAY
ST. VALENTINE'S DAY
PRESIDENTS' DAY
WASHINGTON'S BIRTHDAY
ASH WEDNESDAY

JANUARY
S M T W T F S
1 2 3 4 5 6
7 8 9 10 11 12 13
14 15 16 17 18 19 20
21 22 23 24 25 26 27
28 29 30 31

MARCH
S M T W T F S
1 2 3
4 5 6 7 8 9 10
11 12 13 14 15 16 17
18 19 20 21 22 23 24
25 26 27 28 29 30 31

~ "72 years" ~

Untitled
April – May, 2001
[MSS 0587   43   1]

2:25 : "Nick" phones from San Francisco :
 'hellos' ; talk of "Garden"
 ("ours") ; with 'advice' on
 "what-kind-of 'tomatoes' to plant...
 (suggests "beefsteak", and
 "cherry" ~) . . . .

3PM :
~ eat lunch .
 ~ shortly ; "lie down.."

6PM : ~ "up" :
 ("Nick" has just telephoned ;
 leaves 'message' : "Nothing
 important ~ ; give me a call when
 you have the chance ..."))
 ~ phone Nick :
 (they are not in ...) .

(make "further-entries" ;   ~ Paul (with Margosha ?)
 here ...   has just left .
 ~ at some-time
 (again) : to bed ....))

~ photo : "My Brother In The Snow"
 (~ Holyoke, Mass.)

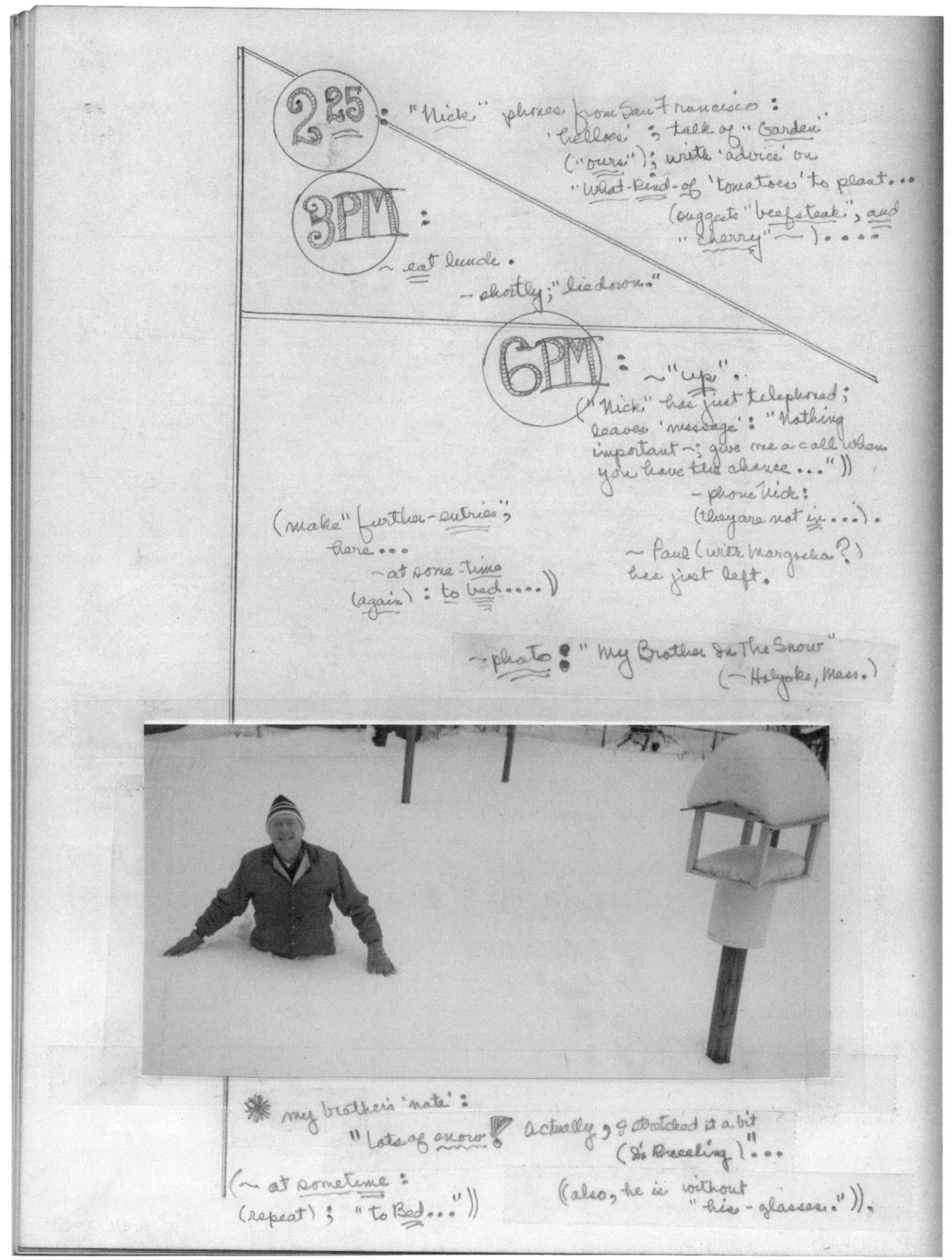

✳ my brother's 'note' :
 "Lots of snow ! Actually, I watched it a bit
 (in breeding)" ...
(~ at sometime :   (also, he is without
(repeat) ; "to Bed..."))   "his-glasses.")).

Untitled
May – June, 2001
[MSS 0587   43   2]

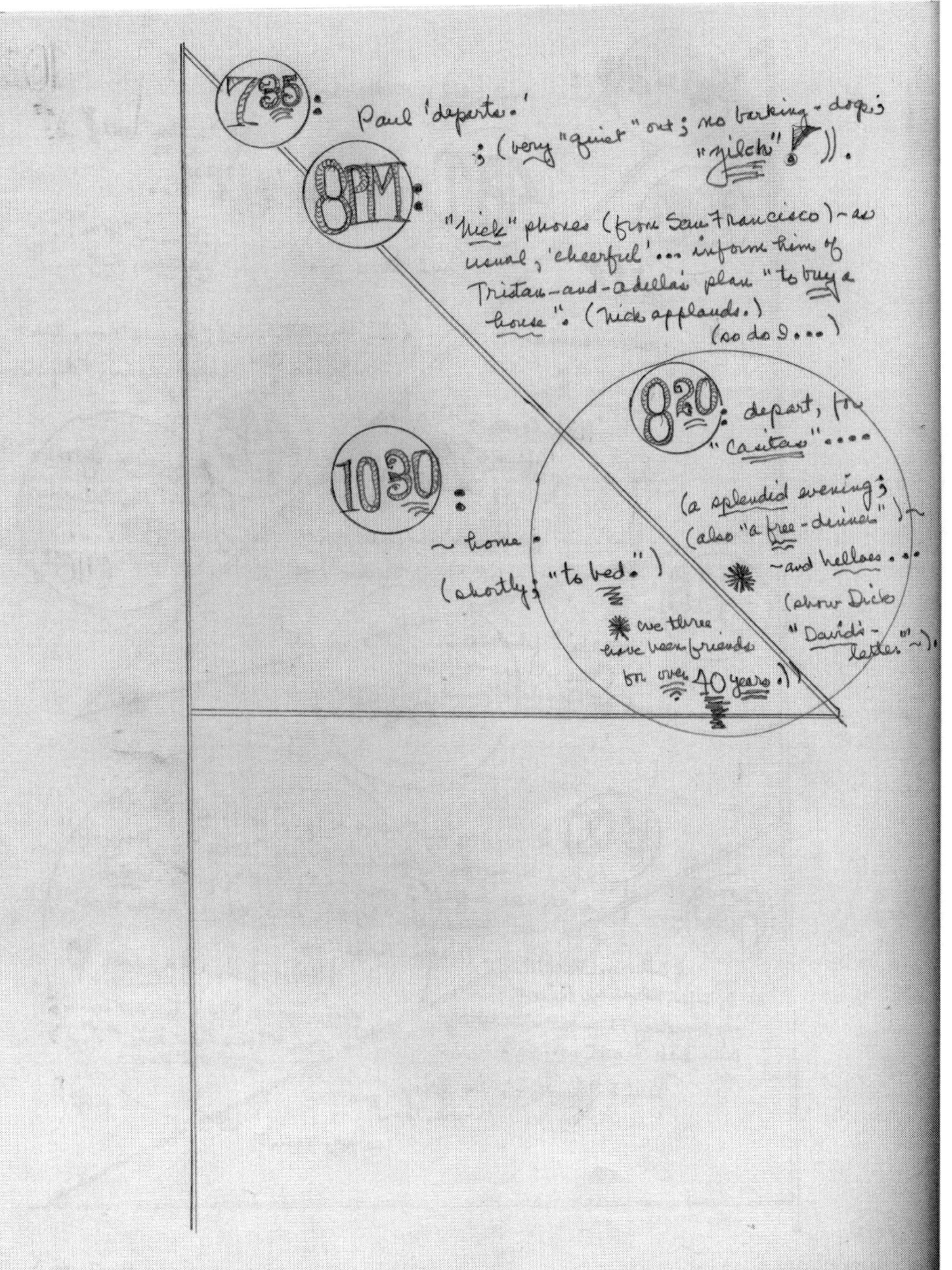

7:35 : Paul 'departs.'
; (very "quiet" out ; no barking-dogs "zilch" !)).
8 PM : "Nick" phones (from San Francisco) — as usual, 'cheerful'... inform him of Tristan-and-Adella's plan "to buy a house". (Nick applauds.)
(so do I...)
8:20 : depart, for "casitas"....
(a splendid evening ; (also "a free-dinner") ~ — and helloes...
(show Dick's "David-letter" ~).
* we three have been friends for over 40 years.)
10:30 : ~ home .
(shortly ; "to bed.")

Untitled
June [2001]
[MSS 0587   43   3]

Sunday June 24th

Up at 7: paper to Paul's
8:15 Paul visits
"sump-pump" has
"gone-out" (water
under house, plus
smell of shit!
I need call
plumber (message
;urgent) to come
tomorrow.
Do so.
*
(made upset)
* plus (earlier
"attack" of some
"food-poisoning"
explosive
vomiting + shits

Untitled
July–August [2001]
[MSS 0587   43   4]

Monday, August 27th — 6

6:10 PM : home from
"little Market"
— Margosha gives
me plate of
(last-night's) pasta
("cold") —; which
I eat —— ("some of")

and "lie?
?? down?"
(I do not)
"lie-down."

12 midnight :

"Tempus-fugit" :
(long-dark; and
getting-darker; have
"Quit" "for-the-Day!"

Untitled
September – November [2001]
[MSS 0587   43   5]

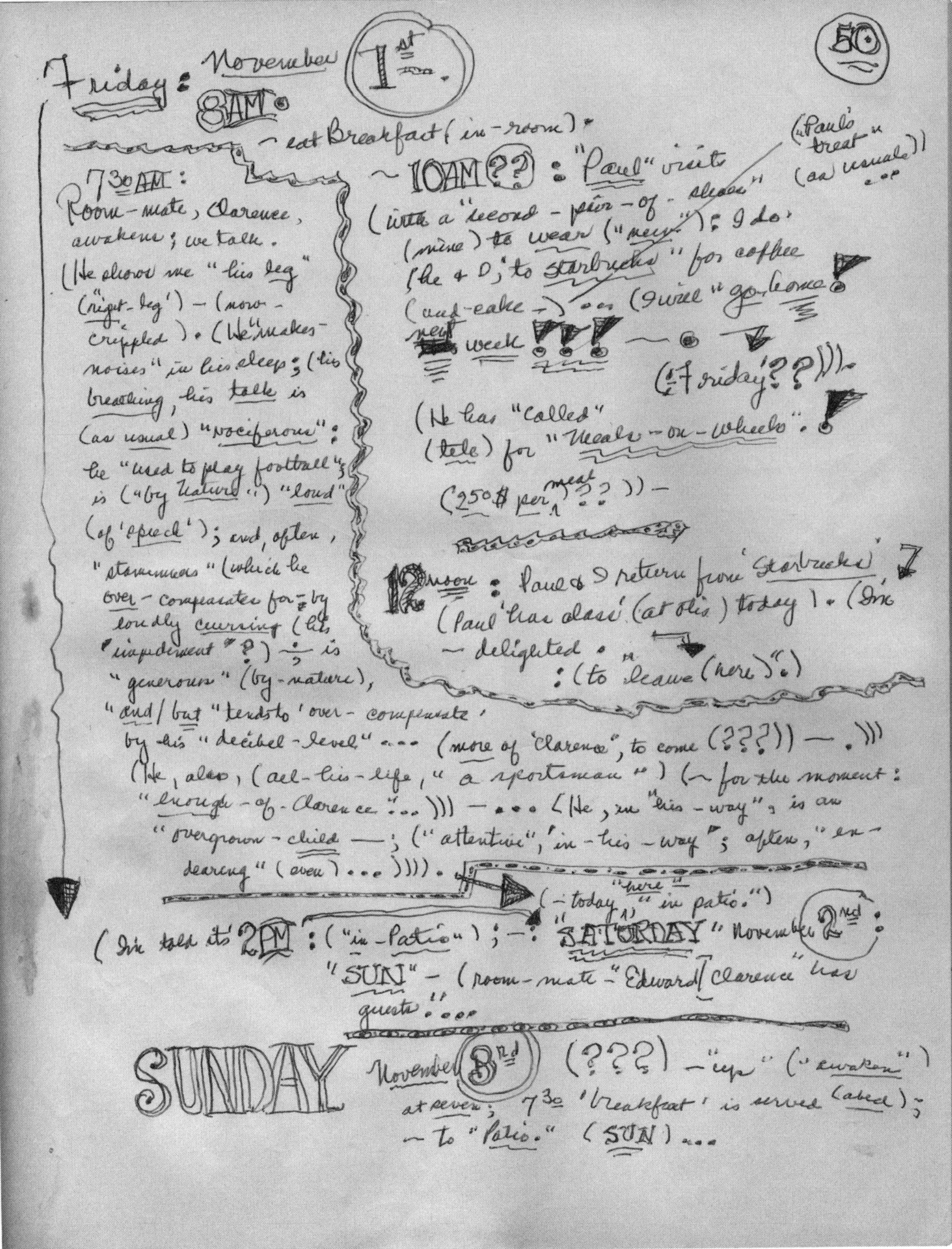

Friday: November **1st**. 50

8AM — eat Breakfast (in-room).

7:30 AM:
Room-mate, Clarence,
awakens; we talk.
(He shows me "his leg"
("right-leg") — (now-
crippled). (He "makes-
noises" in his sleep; (his
breathing, his talk is
(as usual) "vociferous":
he "used to play football";
is ("by nature") "loud"
(of 'speech'); and, often,
"stammers" (which he
over-compensates for — by
loudly cursing (his
"impediment"?) —; is
"generous" (by-nature),
"and/but "tends to 'over-compensate'
by his "decibel-level" ... (more of 'Clarence', to come (???)) — .)))
(He, also, (all-his-life, " a sportsman") (~ for the moment:
"enough-of-Clarence" ...))) — ... [He, in "his-way", is an
"overgrown-child —; ("attentive", "in-his-way"; often, "en-
dearing" (even) ...)))).

~ 10AM ?? : "Paul" visits ("Paul's treat" (as usual))
(with a "second-pair-of-shoes"
(mine) to wear ("new") : I do:
[he + D], to Starbucks" for coffee
(and-cake→) ... (I will "go-leave
next week ??!! ~ . (Friday ???)))-

(He has "called"
(tele) for "Meals-on-Wheels".

(250$ per meal ???))—

12noon : Paul & I return from 'Starbucks'.
(Paul 'has class' (at his) today). (I'm
~ delighted . : (to leave (here)".)

(I'm told its 2PM : ("in-Patio"); —: "SATURDAY" November 2nd : (—today "here" "in patio.")
"SUN" — (room-mate "Edward/Clarence" has
guests" ...

SUNDAY November 3rd (???) — "up" ("awaken")
at seven; 7:30 'breakfast' is served (abed);
~ to "Patio." (SUN) ...

Untitled
November – December [2001]
[MSS 0587   43   6]

Sunday, December 9th — 9th — (5)

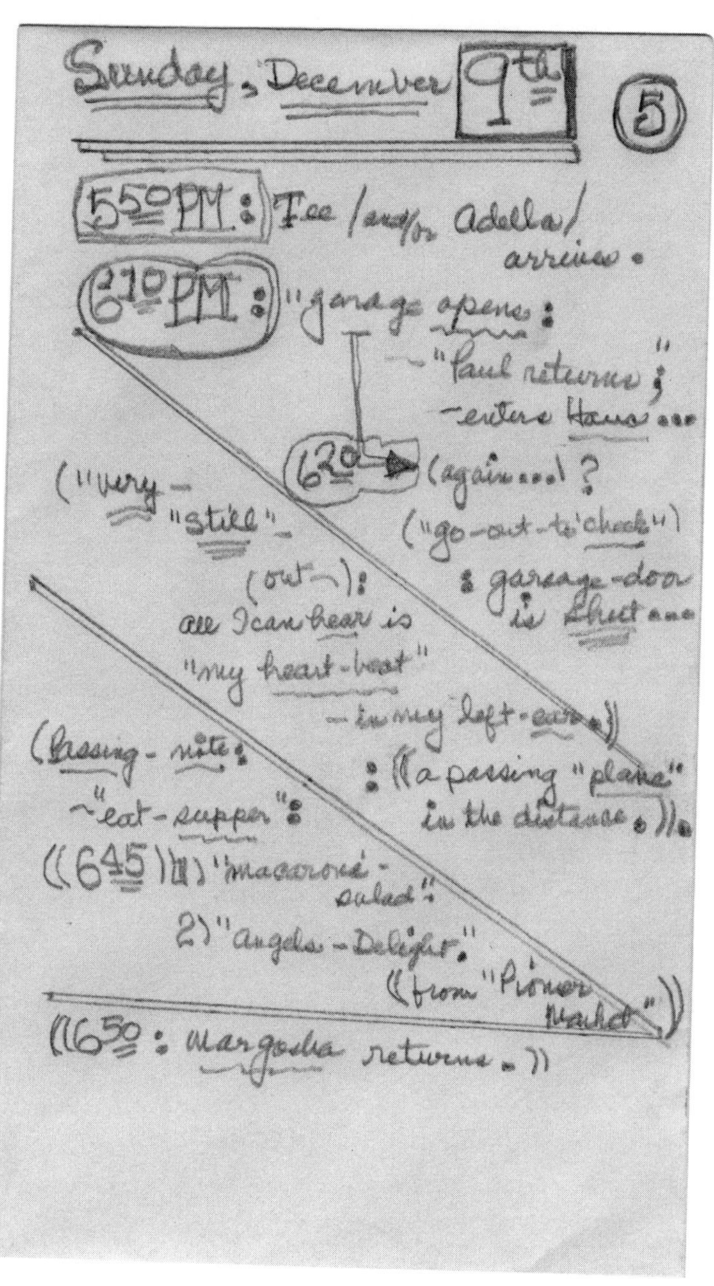

5:50 PM: Tee /and/or Adella/ arrives.

6:10 PM: "garage opens:
→ "Paul returns";
—enters Haus...

6:20 → (again...) ?

("very— "still".

("go-out-to'check")
& garage-door is shut...

(out—):
all I can hear is
"my heart-beat"
—in my left-ear...))

(passing-note: : ((a passing "plane"
"eat-supper":   in the distance.)).

((6:45)III) "macaroni-
                    salad":
        2) "angels-Delight."
                ((from "Pioneer
                        Market"))

((6:50: Margosha returns.))

Other titles from Otis Books / Seismicity Editions

J. Reuben Appelman, *Make Loneliness*
    Published 2008 | 84 pages | $12.95
    ISBN-10: 0-9796177-0-7
    ISBN-13: 978-0-9796177-0-6

Guy Bennett and Béatrice Mousli, Editors, *Seeing Los Angeles:*
    A Different Look at a Different City
    Published 2007 | 202 pages | $12.95
    ISBN-10: 0-9755924-9-1
    ISBN-13: 978-0-9755924-9-6

Jean-Michel Espitallier, *Espitallier's Theorem*
    Translated from the French by Guy Bennett
    Published 2003 | 137 pages | $12.95
    ISBN: 0-9755924-2-4

Norman M. Klein, *Freud in Coney Island and Other Tales*
    Published 2006 | 104 pages | $12.95
    ISBN: 0-9755924-6-7

Ken McCullough, *Left Hand*
    Published 2004 | 191 pages | $12.95
    ISBN: 0-9755924-1-6

Béatrice Mousli, Editor, *Review of Two Worlds:*
    French and American Poetry in Translation
    Published 2005 | 148 pages | $12.95
    ISBN: 0-9755924-3-2

Ryan Murphy, *Down with the Ship*
    Published 2006 | 66 pages | $12.95
    ISBN: 0-9755924-5-9

Hélène Sanguinetti, *Hence This Cradle*
    Translated from the French by Ann Cefola
    Published 2007 | 160 pages | $12.95
    ISBN: 970-0-9755924-7-2

Janet Sarbanes, *Army of One*
    Published 2008 | 173 pages | $12.95
    ISBN-10: 0-9796177-1-5
    ISBN-13: 978-0-9796177-1-3

Severo Sarduy, *Beach Birds*
    Translated from the Spanish by Suzanne Jill Levine and Carol Maier
    Published 2007 | 182 pages | $12.95
    ISBN: 978-9755924-8-9

Adriano Spatola, *Toward Total Poetry*
    Translated from the Italian by Brendan W. Hennessey and Guy Bennett
    with an Introduction by Guy Bennett
    Published 2008 | 176 pages | $12.95
    ISBN: 978-0-9796177-2-0, 0-9796177-3-1

Carol Treadwell, *Spots and Trouble Spots*
    Published 2004 | 176 pages | $12.95
    ISBN: 0-9755924-0-8

Allyssa Wolf, *Vaudeville*
    Published 2006 | 82 pages | $12.95
    ISBN: 0-9755924-4-0

Forthcoming in 2009

Bruce Bégout, *Common Place. The American Motel.*
    Translated from the French by Colin Keaveney

Eric Priestley, *For Keeps.*

Sophie Rachmul, *Los Angeles 1950–1990 – The Emergence of an Artistic Scene
    and of a Poetic Discourse on the City.*
    Translated from the French by Mindy Menjou